THE
URBAN
VEGETABLE
PATCH

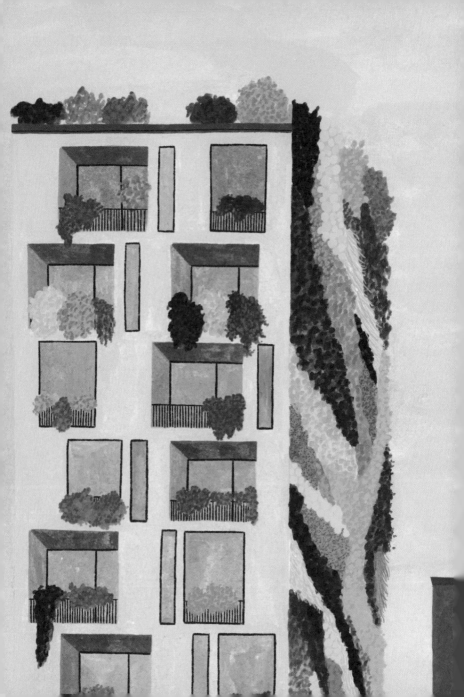

THE
URBAN
VEGETABLE
PATCH

A MODERN GUIDE TO
GROWING SUSTAINABLY,
WHATEVER YOUR SPACE

GRACE PAUL

Hardie Grant

BOOKS

CONTENTS

INTRODUCTION

Like all reputable gardening books, this one starts with a woman in her twenties, with an overdraft, living in an overpriced house-share in a sprawling city, who found happiness by growing vegetables in a variety of spaces. Or something along those lines.

I don't consider myself to be a professional gardener. I'm more a keen amateur – self-taught – who stumbled upon the joy of growing vegetables because I wanted to live more sustainably and save a few pennies towards my non-existent mortgage savings account along the way. Five years on and my mates constantly text me for advice as if I'm some sort of WhatsApp version of a gardening hotline. But so much of what I've learnt has come through trial and error, panicked phone calls to my mum, and our old friend Google. This book captures all that knowledge, gained while growing vegetables everywhere from windowsills to shared gardens to an allotment. I hope these tips and tricks will see you well on your way to growing your own too, and living a happier and hopefully more sustainable life.

We are constantly bombarded by notifications, emails and the latest memes doing the rounds on social media. Did you know that the average person checks their phone 58 times a day? Or that we spend over 8 hours a day looking at a screen? It's exhausting, not to mention the toll it takes on our mental health. I'm sure you're wondering how growing your own vegetables has anything to do with this, but it really does. I can't describe the transformative feeling you can get from tending to plants, taking a step away from technology and focusing on the present – even if only for a few minutes.

The planet we live on is not only crazily busy, it's also in danger. Sorry to bring up the elephant in the room but climate change is real and it's not going away any time soon. I know that tackling it can feel like quite an overwhelming task, but together we can create real change and the sooner we each do our bit, the better. You might find yourself thinking 'what difference will it make if I grow my own vegetables instead of buying them at a supermarket?'. But food production accounts for about a quarter of the world's greenhouse emissions, so growing your own is in fact an instant and direct way to make a big impact on them. Not only that, but you'll be able to avoid food waste by harvesting produce only when you need it – and without the single-use plastic that dominates the fruit and vegetable aisles of shops. All this plastic adds up: according to the United Nations, more than eight million tonnes of the stuff finds its way into our oceans every year, affecting not only animals but humans too. In fact, the average human consumes 50,000 particles of microplastics annually and these particles have been detected in our water: in vegetables, bread and even beer.

You may be concerned about the space you have or the cost of starting up your own vegetable patch. You might live in a shared house, small flat or with your parents. Perhaps you only have a balcony, or are part of a community garden – or maybe you have no space at all. I've experienced all these scenarios and none of them has stopped me growing my own. All the vegetables in this book can be grown in almost any space; you can create your own little oasis, wherever you are.

Lack of cash needn't stop you either. You can turn food tins into plant pots, propagate produce from food scraps you otherwise would have thrown in the bin and swap seeds with people in person or via the internet. And the key thing

– knowledge – is free. Borrow gardening books, explore the wealth of tutorials online and talk to other gardeners: they are a friendly bunch, always willing to share their wisdom.

You might think you need to be green-fingered to grow your own vegetables but this isn't the case. It doesn't matter what your background is or whether you have horticultural genes. Gardening really is for everyone and the vegetables in this book will show you that. It's about learning from your mistakes – there is no shame in getting it wrong. I've witnessed someone destroy a courgette (zucchini) plant by falling on it; I've gone on holiday and left my housemates in charge of my plants, only to come back and discover them dead because nobody watered them; I've 'pruned' a tomato plant by trimming it at the main stem, leaving only a stub. As a wise woman once said, 'you learn from the pain', and lord knows I've felt the pain when I've lifted up a beautiful butternut squash only to see that the other side has been completely eaten by a slug.

On the flip side are the successes. I've grown a melon in a paved garden, seen the joy on my friends' faces when I've given them a bag full of fresh vegetables and experienced the thrill of eating something delicious that I've grown with my own hands. The beauty of gardening is that you're constantly learning and discovering new things while feeling a wonderful sense of serenity and accomplishment – how can you not enjoy that?

This book will teach you to nourish not only yourself, both physically and mentally, but the planet as well. Take care of nature and it will take care of us. Dig in.

1.

WHY YOU SHOULD GROW YOUR OWN

There are so many reasons to grow your own vegetables. Perhaps you want to stick two fingers up to the capitalist element of our current food production system, or maybe the recent global pandemic has got you thinking you might need to be able to produce your own food if the world goes up in flames. Perhaps you like the idea of knowing exactly where your dinner has come from. Or maybe the thought of picking fresh herbs from your windowsill and podding garden-fresh peas simply appeals to you. Whatever your motivation is, I can confirm that it is a good idea.

Here are my top four answers to the question: why do this?

1. FOR THE ENVIRONMENT

Have you ever considered how far the vegetables on your plate have travelled? Yes, some shops use little labels telling you where their produce has come from – but how often do you read and really think about them? In the US, the average distance that produce travels, from farms to tables, is in fact 1,500 miles (2,414 kilometres). That's equal to the distance from Berlin to Cairo or Mexico City to Los Angeles: pretty damn far.

Food production and transportation are huge contributors to climate change and global warming, with the former responsible for one quarter of the world's greenhouse emissions. These industries rely on fossil fuels to power irrigation pumps as well as the machinery that harvests and transports the food – which in turn produces pollution. Pesticide and herbicide distribution also requires fossil fuels and of course can affect the environment.

Fruit and vegetables are the most imported commodity groups in the world: over a third of vegetables in the US are imported and in Britain a massive 75 per cent of fresh produce is brought in from elsewhere. As well as pumping carbon into the atmosphere, that transportation affects the quality and taste of the produce: to enable fresh food to survive the journey, it may be picked when under-ripe, treated with chlorine-based compounds to prolong shelf life or sprayed with ethylene gas to bring on ripeness when required.

Growing your own veg, even a few lettuces on a windowsill, means you have taken one of the biggest steps you can towards reducing your carbon footprint.

2. FOR YOUR WELLBEING

We're slowly becoming slaves to technology, spending several hours a day scrolling through our phones. Millennials are particularly guilty of this, with 87 per cent of them saying their phone never leaves their side. This applies to me, too, (I have to share my veg patch photos online, obviously) but I also know that gardening can provide the respite we need from the technology that constantly bombards us.

According to therapists, doing a bit of gardening has the same positive effect on your brain as going for a walk. In the last few years, doctors have even begun to prescribe gardening as a way to alleviate depression: the fresh air, exercise and connection with others works wonders for some. Community gardens can play a big part in improving people's mental health because they provide spaces where people come together to heal, rebuild and eventually bloom.

Working with your hands and with the earth is very meditative: you can focus solely on the task in the present moment, while becoming more connected with nature and the elements around you. Gardening is an act of hope too: you're giving something a go without knowing whether your seeds or plants will thrive. If they do, however, you'll see results quickly and this can be a major mood boost, showing you what you're capable of and reminding you that you have some control over your environment. A healthy mindset can grow along with your plants, especially if you can consider things as part of a learning curve, rather than failures. Simply ask yourself 'what can I do differently next time?' This kind of process is something we can all benefit from.

Gardening doesn't just help us mentally, it also makes us more active. You'll find yourself doing all sorts of flexible poses as you weed your vegetable patch, and being outdoors is good for our bones as the sun generates vitamin D, which helps us absorb calcium. Coming into contact with soil, meanwhile, exposes us to friendly bacteria that can help support our immune system. So you really are getting a lot out of tending your plants.

Looking at green space out of the window can lower stress and anxiety levels, and being in it. In Japan there's a practice called shinrin-yoku, which means 'forest bathing', that has been proven to have benefits for both body and soul. I'm not suggesting that gardening in a city is the same as wandering in a quiet Japanese forest, but your little vegetable patch can become an oasis of calm where you can immerse yourself after a long day at work.

3. FOR SOCIAL INTERACTION

You might think you don't know any gardeners, but I guarantee that if you bring up the subject, whether it's down the pub or on a dating app, you'll discovers others that are at it too. What's more, since gardeners are often avid enthusiasts, growing your own is a sure-fire way to get conversations going. And, once you've got a few fellow gardeners in your circle, you'll be kept abreast of everything that's going on, not only in their patch but also in neighbouring patches (we are known to enjoy a gossip from time to time down the allotment).

While cities are fantastic places to live, bursting with activities and fun spots to go, they can sometimes be incredibly lonely. You may find yourself living in a shared house where everyone keeps to their rooms. Or you might have moved to a city for a job, leaving friends behind. One way to get around a sense of isolation is to put yourself out there and find new hobbies – gardening being a great one. If you fancy joining a gardening group, you can do so online or in person. Look for a community garden or a local club – try out different ones until you meet the right people for you. It's a brilliant way to make friends and reduce any loneliness you may be feeling. And you'll stumble upon undiscovered green urban gems within the city you're living in, from community gardens hidden away behind busy high streets to horticultural havens flourishing on balconies or roofs high up in the sky.

4. TO SAVE MONEY

One of the arguments I hear most often against gardening is that it's expensive. It's cheaper to buy vegetables at the supermarket, people tell me. But if you have the right information and put in a bit of planning, then this needn't be true at all. OK, you're not going to negate your entire fruit and veg bill by growing your own for the first time, or even the second time – or ever, perhaps. But choose the most cost-effective and high yielding produce such as herbs, lettuce, tomatoes, cucumbers, potatoes, courgettes (zucchini), radishes, (bell) peppers and greens (all featured in the following pages). The more you grow, the more money you'll save and the more self-sufficient you'll become.

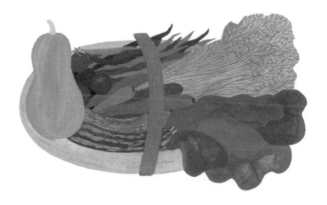

2.
WHAT YOU NEED TO KNOW BEFORE YOU START

Before you head off to the local garden centre ready to splash your hard-earned cash, there are a few things to consider. Have a think about what you want to get out of your veg patch, the best set-up for the space you have and how you can make it as sustainable as possible.

1. WHAT TO GROW

The most important question of all is: what do you like to eat? Obviously, there are a few other things to bear in mind when it comes to growing your own but, overall, it really is as simple as that. Once you've figured that out, have a think about which vegetables taste better to you when they are really fresh versus those you think seem just as good from the shops. For example, we all know nothing beats a tomato fresh from the vine. Potatoes, on the other hand, can be bought locally and cheaply and will probably be as good as home-grown. They're still worth growing, but it makes sense to focus on more unusual varieties that you can't buy. Likewise, you could consider growing unusual squashes, cucamelons or even black tomatoes.

Next, consider your needs. You might want to attempt to produce as many vegetables as you can – perhaps enough to make a significant difference to your food bill. Or you might just fancy growing a few herbs in pots. To be honest, growing too little is probably better than growing too much, at least to start with; you can become overwhelmed by how many plants you've got to look after and you may find yourself sobbing 'what the hell am I meant to do with another glut of courgettes (zuchinni)?'. Slow and steady wins the race; if you're able to, I suggest gradually building up how much you grow as your confidence blooms.

It's vital to consider how much time you have and how much of it you want to dedicate to your plant lords. I don't recommend growing everything in this book all at once – I bloody well wouldn't! I have a job and people to date so I can't be in the garden 24/7 (sorry, plants). However, I can do some watering every evening and spend an hour tending to my plants at the weekend. You might have more time on your hands or more space such as an allotment or a big garden. If this is the case, then you may decide to spend more time there. And, of course, if you're part of a community garden, you'll need to commit time to it as well.

The bulk of the harvest tends to happen during the summer months but, if you are smart about what you grow and focus on vegetables rather than fruit, you can grow throughout the year. This is where salad leaves and herbs come in: they thrive throughout the year indoors. Overwintering vegetables such as alliums (aka leeks, onions, garlic, etc.) will grow outside throughout the colder months. So bear this in mind when you're deciding on what to grow.

2. TOOLS

You may find that the more you grow, the more you're tempted to start shelling out on tools and gadgets. Do you need an irrigation system? Or a watering can sprayer? (Answer: no, they're ridiculous and impossible to handle.) 'Take my money!' you scream at the garden centre, as you decide that a pair of secateurs engraved with your name is essential. Wrong – they aren't. You only need a few basic tools to maintain your vegetable patch. You can do so much with your hands alone – especially if you're growing indoors or in a small space. (I don't even wear gloves but that's just me and it may be why I have non-existent nails.)

For the things you do need, in order to save money and be eco-friendlier, check out second-hand shops and Freecycle. Even better, consider a tool swap with others in a gardening group or perhaps share with your allotment neighbours. If you don't ask, you don't know. (Do agree beforehand that any breakages will be paid for before tools are returned.) If you're buying tools, avoid plastic where you can. Check out equipment made from wood and metal – it will stand the test of time.

BASIC TOOLS

HAND TROWEL: your best friend when it comes to digging and planting. If you have a larger space, you'll also need a full-size spade for the more backbreaking work (there are many joys to only having a small space).

HAND FORK (OR FULL-SIZE GARDEN FORK): perfect for digging up weeds as well as harvesting root vegetables.

HAND RAKE (OR FULL-SIZE RAKE): for smoothing and levelling the surface of the soil.

LABELS: always label your seed pots and seedlings so you know what you've got on the go. You might think a seedling is a nice herb for your windowsill only for it to turn out to be a giant courgette plant that takes over your entire kitchen. This is where labels made from wood, slate or metal come in as they're reusable and will last for years.

GARDEN TWINE: to tie up plants and support them (step away from the plastic cable ties, people).

TWIG CUTTINGS: to support plants. These may be from trees or shrubs you've pruned or ones you have found in your local park. You can also use metal plant supports or wooden canes but twigs are your cheapest option.

SECATEURS: for pruning. Scissors will also work well.

WATERING CAN: do I need to explain this one? See more on watering on pages 32–35, including how to make your own watering appliances.

SAW AND HAMMER: by no means essential but, if you're keen to make your own raised beds or fashion an old pallet into a living wall, I recommend a saw and hammer – maybe even a drill if you're feeling fancy. (Alternatively, rope an elder relative into helping you with this: they will almost certainly have power tools already, as adults do.)

3. SOIL AND COMPOST

Soil is of course a rather important factor when it comes to growing produce. The good news is, that while in time you may become a soil expert and a compost connoisseur – even making your own blends – you can also get along just fine with standard, peat-free ready-made compost as your growing medium. I've certainly had no problems growing vegetables in it. You can buy a specific compost for potting and a multi-purpose one for raised beds and containers.

I wouldn't even think about buying compost that isn't peat-free: peatlands are precious natural habitats and also play a big role in mitigating climate change. They take thousands of years to form but plundering them for peat can destroy them in far less time. In the UK, peatlands have become endangered natural habitats with only 6,000 hectares of bogs remaining: 94 per cent of them have been mined for compost and fuel. A lot of the peat found in composts in the UK is now sourced from other countries and it's our responsibility to protect them, too – so please avoid peat composts at all costs. If the label doesn't clearly state that it's peat-free then it probably isn't. If you're unable to find peat-free compost, alternatives include coir (coconut fibre) and other organic fibres. Keep your eyes peeled for them.

When buying ready-made compost, see if you're able to buy it in a re-usable bag to save on unnecessary single-use plastic – this is becoming a more common option in gardening centres. If you don't have a car, it's a good idea to get your compost delivered from a local gardening centre. Dragging a bag of it around on public transport may be the end of you (be it from exhaustion or from an irate commuter).

You won't need to change the compost in your containers every year, which isn't realistic anyway if you're living in an urban space. As long as you add homemade compost and seaweed fertiliser to your existing compost, you can keep growing in it for years.

If you're growing your vegetables in garden soil rather than in containers, talk to your neighbours, who will be able to inform you of your local soil type and what grows best in it. The same goes for fellow gardeners if you have an allotment or are working at a community garden. Most vegetables in garden soil will benefit from having organic matter, such as food waste compost or well-rotted manure, dug into it or laid on top (which is called mulching – see page 30).

A. HOMEMADE COMPOST

Making your own compost is an efficient way of giving back to the planet all year round. Composting allows you to return food waste to where it came from instead of sending it to landfill. Whether you have a big or small space, creating your own compost will be incredibly worthwhile. Your plants will love it, it helps the soil retain water, and it will keep your shop-bought compost rich and fertile for many a year to come. In fact, when in doubt, add compost – it's like magic for most garden ailments.

The key to making a good compost is to have a 50/50 mix of brown (carbon-rich) and green (nitrogen-rich) materials. If you have too much green material in your bin, it will become slimy and smelly, while too much brown material means it will take ages to break down. There are also certain things you shouldn't put in there at all unless you want your house or garden to smell like the depths of hell.

WHAT YOU CAN PUT INTO YOUR COMPOST BIN...

Green matter: includes fruit and vegetable scraps (be wary of the smellier varieties, such as onions and garlic, if you're using a compost bin indoors), tea bags (check that they're plastic-free!), eggshells, coffee grounds, hair, manure, weeds (without seed heads) and grass clippings.

Brown matter: cardboard, paper, dry leaves, sawdust and wood chippings.

...AND WHAT YOU CAN'T

Cooked food, dairy products, meat, fish, bones and excrement – all of these will cause a rotten smell and potentially attract rats and other vermin. You don't want to have to call the exterminator out because of a compost bin.

Top compost bin tips

- Stir your compost every week to get air into it and aid decomposition.

- Cut up the scraps you put into the bin: the smaller they are, the quicker they'll decompose.

- If your bin starts to smell, add more brown matter. This will soak up the moisture in the compost and the smell along with it.

- If you have excess compost, you can ask any gardening friends if they'd like it or drop it off at a compost collection point.

- If you want to get your hands on more scraps to add to your bin, speak to housemates, friends and, if you're ballsy enough, local restaurants and supermarkets about their fruit and veg waste.

HOW TO MAKE YOUR OWN COMPOST BIN

You don't need lots of space for your own compost bin – in fact you can use one that fits into a kitchen cupboard – and you can create your own or buy a specifically designed indoor compost bin. If you have a bigger space, you can fashion one outside using objects such as pallets, a plastic or metal bin, a crate – even an old drawer. The key thing is to have a lid; so if your container doesn't have one already, fashion something out of wood or heavy canvas.

What you'll need
- Container
- Something to make holes in the container, such as scissors, hammer and nails or a drill
- Tray that fits underneath the container
- 2–4 sheets newspaper
- Soil or compost, enough to cover the bottom of your container by about 10 cm (4 in)

1. Make holes in the side and the base of the container. This is to ensure that the compost gets enough oxygen to aid decomposition.

2. Line the tray with a couple of sheets of newspaper and put the container on top of it. The tray will catch any liquid that might come out of it, aka bin juices. The official term for this liquid is leachate. If it's brown and odourless, you can use it as a fertiliser by diluting it one part leachate to ten parts water. However, don't use it if it's smelly and yellow as it could potentially harm your plants.

3. Fill the first 10 cm (4 in) of your container with soil or bought compost. Shred one or two sheets of newspaper and lay this on top of the soil.

4. Start adding your food and garden scraps. Be patient; they can take six months to a year – sometimes longer – to turn into compost. You'll know your compost is ready when it has an earthy quality and the original contents are no longer recognisable. When it reaches this stage, leave it for a few more weeks so it fully decomposes before using it around your plants.

B. FERTILISER

While compost feeds the soil; fertiliser feeds the plants. One of the many reasons to grow your own veg is that you'll know exactly what they've been grown in and exactly what's been used on them. Most of the plants in this book will do just fine without fertiliser but it will give them a boost if you use it; some may need more of a helping hand than others. Inorganic fertilisers, made from synthetic materials, cause a lot of damage to the soil, the planet and those who inhabit it due to the chemicals they contain, so please buy organic ones. A wide array of them are readily available, made from animal and vegetable products, including poultry manure, alfalfa, seaweed and nettles.

You don't need to spend a fortune on different fertilisers. An organic tomato feed will do the job for many fruiting plants, including courgettes (zucchini) and beans. Once you see the fruit start to emerge, feed the plants every 2 weeks to help them on their way. Organic liquid seaweed is a great micronutrient-rich pick me up too: giving it to your plants once a month will make a big difference. We all live busy lives and remembering to feed your plants might sound like a bit of a faff, but you can set up a recurring alert on your phone to do the remembering for you.

C. NO-DIG GARDENING

If you are one of the lucky people who have a larger outside space with grass and soil, then congratulations, you have a golden ticket. Bigger space comes with bigger responsibilities, though, and can mean more weeding, so it's not all fun and games. However, there is a way to create a really productive vegetable patch that requires no digging at all. What is this madness, I hear you cry?! But yes, it's true.

There are many benefits to no-dig gardening, apart from not breaking your back. For a start, turning over the soil releases carbon into the atmosphere, something we definitely want to avoid. And secondly, soil is a complex ecosystem teeming with life and every time you dig a fork into it, you're disturbing it. By not digging, you're encouraging it to do its own thing and become more fertile, which in turn makes it more productive when you grow plants in it. The idea is to mimic the soil in natural habitats such as forests, where the soil is covered with plants, leaves and twigs that fall to the ground and eventually decompose.

You can emulate this in your own space by mulching, which means covering the soil with organic material to enrich it. Mulching also deprives weeds of light so you'll be reducing them as well, which will save you time. No digging is required of you – leave that to the worms.

You can start a no-dig patch by creating a raised bed with wood, bricks or even tyres and filling it with compost. You'll be able to start sowing plants into it immediately. If you don't want to go down the raised bed route, you can turn a weed-infested bit of ground, or even just a patch of grass, into a plot that's ready to plant in straight away by following the instructions opposite.

HOW TO CREATE A NO-DIG VEGETABLE PATCH

You'll need
Plain brown carboard (you can also use well-rotted manure or straw)
Multi-purpose ready-made compost

1. Cover your patch of weedy ground or grass with a layer of cardboard, ensuring there are no gaps for the light to get in: darkness is needed to kill any weeds that are causing havoc.

2. Soak the cardboard with water, to help it break down quicker, and cover with a layer of compost, about 20 cm (8 in) deep, patting it down so the surface is fully covered.

3. You can plant straight away into the compost or you can leave it for a few months for the carboard to decompose. If weeds do emerge, cover them with more cardboard and compost – or you can pick them by hand but be careful not to disturb the soil too much.

4. You will only need to 'build' your patch once. After your first season, you can keep on top of weeds by covering the ground with more organic material, such as homemade compost, once you've harvested your crop. This will allow the soil to enrich further during the colder months.

4. SUSTAINABLE GARDENING

There are many ways you can garden. You can go down the chemical route, which I do not recommend, and which would contradict everything I've said and will continue to say in this book. Or you can be mindful of the planet when you're cultivating the vegetable patch of your dreams.

Keep in mind the following things and you can make a difference not only to yourself but to your environment.

A. WASTE-AWARE WATERING

Sorting out your watering set-up is one of the most important things you need to do when starting your own patch. Mains water tends to be the go-to choice for most of us as it's readily available and reliable. But it can add up in terms of cost, and it's not great for the environment as excessive water extraction can affect the quality and quantity of freshwater systems, endangering flora and fauna in the process. So get your pots and pans out and collect water that's free, isn't metered and isn't full of chemicals. Need I say more?

RAINWATER: if you have a larger space, then look into getting a water butt – be it a shop-bought one or a repurposed one such as an old beer barrel – and install it on the downpipes of your house (the pipes that run down from the roof). Make sure it's covered with a lid to avoid any creepy crawlies making it their own personal hot tub. If you don't have space for a water butt, you can simply place a bucket underneath your gutter to collect the water. And if you don't have a gutter, put out some containers, such as old takeaway boxes, and wait for the rain to come. Once you've collected the water, cover it with a lid so it doesn't evaporate or start to smell until you wish to use it.

How to make your own watering sprinkler

If you're gardening indoors, I'd suggest getting a plastic bottle and making some holes in the lid. You can fill the bottle up, put the lid on and voila, you have a little sprinkler. Thrifty.

How to get water directly to the roots

When you're watering, it's best to pour the water around the base of the plant to avoid it going all over the leaves and potentially not making it down to the roots. This will save water as well. If you're growing vegetables that really need water to their roots, you can cut the bottom off a large plastic bottle before burying it, neck down, next to the plant. Pour water directly into the bottle and it will make its way to the roots quicker.

GREY WATER: this is the term for water that's already been used in the house, including bath and shower water, washing up water and washing machine water (toilet water doesn't come under this category, in case you had any wild thoughts). Normally it would just go down the drain but you can use it to water your plants. You can collect it using a diverter, a device that connects to your pipes and sends water to a water butt, but there's nothing wrong with scooping it straight from the bath or sink: it works just as well. Water containing household soaps won't cause any damage to your plants, but bleach and stronger cleaning products including floor and window cleaners will, so be wary of that. You wouldn't want to be responsible for chemically destroying your plants. Unlike rainwater, grey water should be used right away to avoid any smells, and it's best not to use it on plants such as herbs that will be eaten without being cooked. (Unless you like the taste of herbs seasoned with soap.)

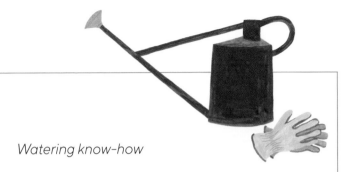

Watering know-how

- The best time to water your plants is first thing in the morning, or in the evening before sunset (unless you're up for watering in the dark with a headlamp on). This minimises the evaporation of the water so your plants get the maximum benefit and you waste less.

- A soil rich in compost will be great at retaining water. So if you're growing in garden soil, make sure it has some compost dug in.

- In the 'Time to thrive' section of each vegetable project in chapter four, I give you advice on how much water the plant needs (though every plant is different, as is your set-up, so this may vary). It's very easy to smother our plant babies with too much, drowning them and wasting water. When in doubt, stick your finger into the soil: if it feels dry, then it's time to give your plants some liquid love. If the soil is damp, you can carry on with your day. Of course, if you're experiencing a freak heatwave, then water your plants twice a day as a precaution.

B. PESTS

One of the best things about growing your own is that you can sleep easy at night knowing your plants haven't been sprayed with an array of chemicals. Pesticides are not only bad for us, for animals and for the planet but they're also harmful to the beneficial insects that help keep our ecosystems healthy.

You may be thinking that you won't need pest control for a small patch outside, but let me tell you: you should never underestimate slugs and snails. They will go to untold lengths to crush your soul by destroying your vegetables without a shred of remorse. Greenfly, blackfly and caterpillars also like to cause havoc.

But you do have plenty of sustainable options for pest control. You can go down an entirely natural route or explore organically certified repellents which will also do the job.

NATURAL PEST CONTROL
This means banishing the bad guys by purely physical and/or completely chemical-free means.

Water spraying: a good jet of water can go a long way when it comes to bugs such as aphids (greenfly), in the garden. Blast them off leaves and stems when you see them and they should eventually get the message that they're not welcome.

Hand picking: this is not exactly the quickest or most pleasant of tasks, but you can hand-pick larger offending creatures off your plants. Slugs and snails seem to have a homing instinct and could be back before you know it (I told you they're sneaky) so take them somewhere far from home, such as the vegetable patch of your worst enemy.

Insects: if you encourage certain helpful insects or other creatures into your space they will take care of pests for you, largely by eating them for breakfast. The good guys get a meal and you won't have to watch your plants be destroyed – everyone's a winner. One way to lure them in is by installing an insect hotel to make your patch inviting (page 44). A water feature is a good option too (page 43).

Companion planting: is another great way to either repel certain pests or draw in other insects that will eat them. You can even have 'sacrificial' plants, such as nasturtiums, that courageously lure pests away from their neighbours. The most effective companion plants are:

- *Basil*: aphids can be a real pain and rather stubborn when you ask them to leave so plant some basil amongst your tomatoes to repel them. Plus, you can eat the basil so you get two for the price of one.
- *Coriander (cilantro)*: this beauty's scent repels aphids and carrot fly. It also tastes delicious and I won't hear otherwise.
- *Marigolds*: these deter aphids as well as white fly from beans, plus they'll add a pop of colour to your vegetable patch.

- *Lavender*: I realise that the word lavender may conjure up images of old talc gift boxes, but hear me out as it's pretty great. Not only will its scent attract pollinators – the insects we really want in our space – but it will repel the ones we don't want such as mosquitoes and flies (even scorpions, though I've never had that issue funnily enough). It's sort of like a veg patch bouncer.

- *Garlic chives*: this is another two-for-the-price-of-one plant. Not only do they taste delicious, but they repel carrot fly as well as aphids.

Barriers and deterrents: I'm not suggesting here that you surround your vegetable patch with barbed wire, but there are some effective ways of diverting certain pests.

- *Coffee grounds and broken eggshells*: instead of throwing them into the bin, scatter a thick layer of either of these around plants to stop slugs and snails from crawling over them. It's the natural equivalent of barbed wire.

- *Netting*: if you have a bigger space, then you'll be dealing with larger pests and birds. I was at war with a neighbouring cat for an entire summer as he rather enjoyed digging up my plants, destroying my hard work within the space of a few hours and leaving a nice big poo behind as a treat. Eventually I decided to pull out the big guns and covered my plants with netting. Not ideal but it did the job.

- *CDs*: we all have a collection of CDs that we keep saying we're going to take to the charity shop but we never do. Put them to good use by hanging them up in your vegetable patch to deter birds, especially our pigeon friends. If you have a bigger space, you could go all out and create a scarecrow to save you from you having to patrol your patch during the day like some sort of vigilante.

MAKING A WILDLIFE-FRIENDLY SPACE

Wildlife habitats are disappearing at an alarming rate around the globe due to increased housing, deforestation, climate change and many other cheerful factors. By making small changes to your veg patch, whatever its size, you'll be able to do your bit to counteract this habitat loss, creating a home for certain creatures, providing them with shelter, food, and a five-star pad to hibernate in during the colder months. Some creatures are more useful than others – for example, at the allotment I help out at, there's a resident fox called One Eye (I'm sure you can guess why). One of her favourite activities is digging up potatoes, in the dead of night, at the precise moment they're ready to be harvested. Thankfully, foxes are not among the creatures who will be encouraged to move into your patch by the suggestions below:

FLOWERS: flowers and flowering herbs are an ideal way to attract pollinators. These critters are essential for our ecosystems and for biodiversity. Bees are the top pollinators, yet the number of them around the world is declining fast due to chemicals, climate change and intensive farming practices that lead to habitat loss. If things carry on as they are, certain species of plants may become extinct. You can encourage bees, and other pollinators, to drop by and pollinate your vegetables, whatever your space.

Windowsill and ledges: herbs are ideal for these spaces but will only benefit pollinators if you allow them to flower. Normally you'd pinch off the flowers to optimise flavour in the leaves – but let a few of them flower to help pollinators out.

- *Flowers*: sweet pea, alpine aster, cornflower, wallflower, scabious, winter pansy
- *Herbs*: sage, basil, chervil, lavender, oregano, thyme

Balconies, roof terraces and paved areas: these spaces offer so many growing opportunities for herbs, flowers and even small bushes. You can use containers, be it pots or hanging baskets, or you could create a living wall (pages 74–75). If your space is very exposed, such as a high-rise balcony or a roof terrace, make sure you use hardier varieties that withstand harsher conditions, especially wind. I'd suggest putting up a screen of some sort to provide protection.

- *Flowers*: sweet pea, wallflower, sweet William, yarrow, catnip
- *Bushes and climbers*: heather, skimmia, potentilla, jasmine
- *Herbs*: sage, basil, mint, lemon verbena, borage, fennel
- *Wind-friendly plants*: pollinators don't like windy conditions so use bamboo and needle grasses where possible to offer shelter.

Gardens and allotments: minimise close-mown lawn where possible or leave a patch untouched so pollinators can create their own little oasis. Get some climbing plants going up the walls, fill pots and containers and put up hanging baskets. Your garden will be teeming with pollinators before you know it. You might have a larger outside space, such as an allotment, where you can plant fruiting hedges and trees.

- *Flowers*: wallflower, poppy, allium, lavender, honeysuckle, foxgloves
- *Trees*: apple, cherry, maple, hazel

BIRDS: if you have a larger outdoor space, put a bird box high up in a sheltered area and hang up a bird feeder or two. Watch out for squirrels though as they love bird feed and, for the love of God, don't throw out bread in your space unless you want rats to move in.

WATER: a water-filled feature, from a little bird bath up to a full-scale pond, will bring birds and insects to your yard. Some of these helpful visitors will tackle pests; frogs, for example, are the best slug-killers in town.

INSECT HOTEL: this nifty creation will encourage insects such as ladybirds and green lacewings to move in and they, in turn, will help get rid of pests working their way through your vegetable patch. You can easily make your own using a container, such as a wooden box, turned on its side – whatever size works for your space – filled with natural materials including leaves and twigs, with a roof to ensure it remains relatively dry. I'm assuming you wouldn't want to sleep in a wet bed and neither do our insect friends.

D. SEED AND PLANT SEEDS SWAPS

These are exactly what they say imply: an opportunity to swap seeds and plants, as well as knowledge, with fellow gardeners. This sort of exchange has been going on for years over garden fences and at local gardening clubs, and it's gaining momentum again. It's a great way to pass on excess plants that you no longer need and gain some that you would like to trial.

Swaps are a great way to save money and reduce 'plant miles' – aka the distance seeds or plants travel to get to your garden. You're also likely to pick up seeds or plants that you hadn't considered growing before. Be careful though: don't be lured into getting plants you genuinely don't need, no matter how nice the other gardener is. It's worth having a plan in mind before you go or drawing up a list of what you need. If not, you could come home with five rare chilli plants that die within a week because you don't live in a tropical jungle. And you may need to hone your haggling skills to make sure you're not losing out.

Swaps can be organised by gardening communities, online, via the post or even among a group of friends. It's as simple as deciding what you'd like to swap and getting on with it. The events are normally free, although some may have a fundraising element to them so donate a few pennies if you can.

How to collect your own seeds

Preserving seeds from plants you've already grown is a cost-effective way of ensuring you have seeds for next season or that you can swap for others. It's simple to do and I've flagged the plants you can do this with throughout the book:

1. Extract the seeds from your plant. With some vegetables, such as beans, leave the pods to dry on the plant before removing them. With lettuces or herbs, allow them to flower and then form seed heads. To get seeds from fruits such as tomatoes, scoop the juicy part with the seeds into a sieve and hold under running water until you're left with just the seeds.

2. If they haven't dried on the plant, leave your seeds to dry on a sunny windowsill. Once they're dry, store them in a clearly labelled and dated jar or envelope in a cool, dry place. They can last from 2–5 years depending on the conditions they're stored in: avoid exposing them to light, heat and high humidity as this will shorten their shelf life.

E. SUSTAINABLE CONTAINERS AND FURNITURE

Instead of spending money on pots or garden furniture, try to re-use, recycle and upcycle when possible. This will not only save you a few pennies and help the environment, but will also make your space unique. You can create a lot out of very little, from turning egg boxes (cartons) into seed trays to making someone else's rubbish into the perfect furniture for your patch. Channel your inner design guru and convert a pallet into a living wall (pages 74–75), brighten up rusty old pots with a lick of paint – the world is your oyster. Check out the bric-a-brac that people leave outside their homes, or turn to eBay, Freecycle, Facebook Marketplace and Gumtree for local furniture that is in need of a new home.

If you are buying new garden furniture, choose eco-friendly materials and look for the Forestry Stewardship Council (FSC) certified logo on wooden products. The FSC police illegal logging, deforestation and poor working practices in the timber industry. Also check the origins of the furniture: try to buy locally if possible, to cut down on transportation costs. You'd be surprised how much you can source locally when you start doing a little research.

MAKE YOUR OWN CONTAINERS

You may think that starting your own vegetable patch means you'll have to buy all the pots and gear to go in it. But put the credit card away: use a little creativity and you can easily make your own containers at no cost.

For sowing seeds

As long as they have drainage, plants aren't too fussy about what they're grown in: you'll be much more concerned about what the container looks like than they are. The following household objects make great starter homes for seeds where they'll quickly flourish into seedlings:

- *Egg boxes (cartons)*: these are the best seed trays in town. Fill each cup with compost and plant your seeds into them direct. When the seedlings are ready to be planted out, you can divide up the cups and plant each module into the ground directly. The dream.

- *Yoghurt pots (cartons) and tins (cans)*: two household objects that are incredibly versatile and can be used for an array of purposes including as vessels for seeds. Wash them out when you've finished with them and make a few holes in the base to create drainage. You can pop gross-looking plastic pots inside tins to make them more appealing. To avoid water gathering at the bottom, put a handful of stones in first so the pot doesn't sit in a pool of water.

- *Toilet roll tubes*: these are biodegradable so once your seedling is ready to be planted out, you can just put the whole thing into the ground, saving time – my favourite kind of gardening. To make your own toilet roll pot, flatten the tube to create two creased edges. Open it up, turn it 90 degrees and flatten it again so you create two more creased edges. When you open it up, you will have a square tube. Cut about 2.5 cm (1 in) into each crease to create four flaps at the end of the tube. Moving in a clockwise direction, fold each of the flaps down and voila, you have a biodegradable pot!

- *Newspaper pots*: another biodegradable container for seedlings. All you need is some newspapers and a cylindrical object, such as a rolling pin or a bottle, to wrap the paper around as a mould. Turn the ends in using the method mentioned above.

- *Guttering*: this is a little more adventurous, but you can cut guttering to the perfect length for your space so it's worth the effort. Once you've decided on the right length, tape over the ends and fill with soil. Plant your seeds directly into the soil; when ready to plant out, un-tape one of the ends, push the half-cylinder of soil out of the guttering and either 'break off' individual plants or dig a trench and slide the whole row of plants into it.

- *Sturdy carrier bags*: these are particularly good for growing potatoes – again, make sure there are drainage holes in the bottom.

- Other suggestions include old drawers, bins, buckets – anything you can put some compost in really.

Larger plants and raised beds

If you've got a bigger space, then containers and raised beds are your friends. They're a great way to grow vegetables if you have a paved area, or you want to dedicate only a certain part of your garden to growing. Or you might have an alley that you can convert from dead space into a patch with a few containers or raised beds. They're versatile, you can move them around and you can take them with you when you move to a new house (and if you're renting in a city, that tends to be once a year when your lease is up). I've carted my raised beds to three different properties and they're still going strong after 5 years.

Instead of forking out for expensive containers, create your own by upcycling objects that would otherwise go to waste:

- *Tyres*: these are among the biggest polluters on the planet as they take so long to break down. But fill a tyre with compost and, hey presto, you have a raised bed. You can stack them, you can use them as the edges for a larger raised bed, you can even use them to create a path in your space.

- *Bricks and logs*: you can create the edges of raised beds easily with these, working to whatever shape and size works best for you.

- *Buckets*: not only useful for water, these also make great containers for many a plant.

- *Pallets*: if you live in a city then you will no doubt have gone to some trendy rooftop bar – probably on top of a disused car park because why the hell not – that had tables made out of pallets. You can emulate this vibe at home, if the fancy takes you, or you can ignore my hipster comment and use a pallet to create a living wall – see pages 74–75 – or a raised bed.

- *Cardboard boxes*: hold a few back from the recycling bin and fill with soil or compost to convert into a temporary home for your plants that should last one season. Once you've finished with them, add to your home compost bin.

- *Old bathtub*: many people have mentioned these to me as being great for the garden. I've yet to stumble upon an old bathtub myself – I've rarely lived in a rented house that actually had a useable bath, let alone one going spare. But if you ever come by one and don't know what to do with it, turn it into a funky plant container.

F. EXCESS HARVEST

Once you've started growing and are beginning to get the hang of things, you might find yourself with a glut on your hands: more produce than you can handle. Don't even think about throwing it away or leaving it to rot – not today, Satan. Here are some things you can do if you have more tomatoes than you can shake a stick at:

PRESERVE: this may become a necessary skill if you find yourself expanding your vegetable patch over time, but even with a small plot, it is a wonderful way to make the most of your produce for later. You have complete control over what ingredients you use with your vegetables too. You can pickle vegetables (pages 123 and 146), turn them into sauces (pages 91, 104, 140–141 and 163), blitz them into delicious soups, blanch them so that will keep in the freezer for the colder months, or even dry them. There is no need to waste anything.

GIVE IT AWAY: I can confirm that giving fresh vegetables to other people is a sure-fire way to win them over. Alternatively you can have a free stand outside your home or in your block of flats. Put whatever produce you don't need into a box and add a little sign specifying that it's free. Also, you get a gold star for being so wholesome.

DONATE: local food banks, nursing homes and shelters may be very happy to take homegrown vegetables – though do check beforehand that they accept fresh produce as some places may not.

SELL: you could become quite the entrepreneur and sell your produce. Unless you're in it to make your millions, I'd recommend setting up a take what you need/pay what you can system. The money that you raise can go towards next season's seeds and any tools you may need for your plot, especially if you decide to upscale it.

G. COOKING

We all know that the best part of growing your own vegetables is being able to eat them. It's one of the main reasons to do it, right? And the more homegrown vegetables you eat, the more sustainable your cooking will be. Here are some planet-friendly kitchen tips to complement your sustainable gardening:

ROOT TO SHOOT: not all the leaves, tops and trimmings of vegetables need to go straight in the compost; many can be turned into delicious dishes. Experiment with them: try sautéing beetroot (beet) leaves with a little oil and garlic, creating a vegetable stock with carrot, onion and celery trimmings, coating root veg peelings with oil and baking into crisps (chips) or making carrot tops into a delicious pesto.

REDUCE FOOD WASTE: we waste an awful lot of food, and in Britain 95 per cent of it ends up in landfill. Here, because it doesn't receive any oxygen, it produces methane, one of the most potent greenhouse gases. When composting at home, on the other hand, the waste is exposed to oxygen so produces carbon dioxide (which is far less potent). So plan your meals ahead of time to avoid buying surplus ingredients and make sure you use scraps wisely (see above) or put them in a food recycling bin. Get into the habit of adapting recipes and experimenting: flexible cooking is one of the best ways to avoid waste and helps you use everything you have in your fridge.

5. HOW TO PLANT

So you've got all the information you need and you're ready to start growing vegetables, but there's the slight issue of having no idea how to start off seeds or transplant seedlings once they've grown. Don't worry, I've got you covered: it's a doddle.

A. SEEDS

Some people think that growing from seed, rather than buying young plants, can be a faff. Yes, it can and yes, seeds can be bloody fickle sometimes. But it's worth it: it's more economical than buying seedlings and the satisfaction of growing your own plants from scratch is fantastic. If you don't have the time and space to grow from seed, though, go with seedlings – you do you.

A word of warning: when sowing seeds, don't be overzealous. It's very easy to get carried away and then find yourself with hundreds of lettuce plants, never wanting to look at a salad again. You should always plant a few more seeds than you need, to compensate for any casualties, but not hundreds.

You can grow seeds in whatever container you have to hand, from small pots to large seed trays. For the former, I recommend egg boxes (cartons) (page 48).

Check the instructions on the packet regarding the spacing of the seeds and the conditions they require – both of which vary depending on what you're growing. Grab some ready-made compost and fill your seed container nearly to the top. Depending on the variety, you might need to sprinkle the seeds on the surface and cover them with a light dusting of compost or you might have to make a hole with your finger and drop the seeds into it before covering them up. After sowing, water and place in a warm, sunny spot. Keep an eye out to check that the compost doesn't dry up – it should be kept moist, but not too wet – and that your seeds don't burn alive due to excessive sun. You don't want to fall at the first hurdle.

Some seeds need warmer conditions than others to germinate. This is when something called a propagator comes into play. Propagators are mini incubators that trap heat inside, creating warm and constant conditions for the seeds to germinate.

Eventually your patience will pay off and the magic will begin to happen: you'll notice a little shoot poking through the compost. Congratulations, your seeds are beginning to germinate, which means you've achieved step one with flying colours. How long germination takes depends on what you're growing: shoots can appear within a matter of days or can take a few weeks.

Be patient: if nothing seems to be happening after it should have, give them an extra week so they can prove their worth. If nothing happens, then it just wasn't meant to be. It could be because the seeds were old, they were sown too deep or, if planted outside, they have been eaten.

Seeds failing to germinate happens to the best of us and is all part of the adventure. It happened to me recently with some thyme seeds that I'd had kicking around for a while. You can try again, or you can get yourself down to the gardening centre and buy some seedlings so you can magically progress to the next stage. Don't worry, I won't tell anybody – mainly because I've done it myself more times than I care to remember.

How to make a DIY propagator

You will need
Egg box (carton)
Tray
Seeds
A transparent 'roof' (such as a fruit punnet)
Ready-made compost
Tape

1. Fill the cups of the egg box with compost and plant your seeds as per the instructions on the packet. Water so the compost is moist.

2. Put the egg box on the tray and put the 'roof' over the top of it. If you're using a punnet and there are holes in it, cover them with clear tape to trap the heat in. Voila, you have a propagator.

B. SEEDLINGS

You may have grown your seedlings with your own fair hands, or you may have bought them. The latter option is a real blessing if you don't have the time or space, or just can't be arsed, to grow plants from seeds. Seedlings are readily available at garden centres and supermarkets as well as online and through plant swaps.

If you've acquired seeds from elsewhere and you want to plant them outside, you'll need to check they've been 'hardened off'. This also applies to seedlings that you've grown yourself. Hardening off means getting your plants used to the outdoor environment, which can be quite a shock for seedlings that have grown in a lovely indoors cocoon, safe from wind, rain, frost and pests. If you put them straight outside, they're not going to be happy at all. To harden them, put them outside during the day and bring them in at night for about a week so they can grow acclimatised to the outside world. Once you've done this, they'll be ready for the big move.

Planting seedlings into a larger space, whether a container inside or outside or straight into the ground, is simple but it can be rather painstaking work if you have a lot of seedlings. As you slowly work your way through them, cursing how many seeds you rather optimistically decided to sow (don't say I didn't warn you), remind yourself of the mental benefits of gardening (pages 12–14).

To plant, first dig a hole as deep as the pot the seedling is currently in. If you're planting directly into soil and want to give your seedling an extra boost, add a handful of compost. Water the hole. Lightly spray or water your seedling in its pot to make it easier to get out. Pop the plant out by pushing up on the base of the container with your fingers. If it's being stubborn, turn the pot upside down, support the plant with one hand and give the base of the pot a sharp tap with a hand trowel – that should do the job. Gently loosen the roots and the soil ball that has formed: be careful, do not fall at this hurdle by destroying the roots as you'll never forgive yourself. Pop your plant into the hole. (If you're using biodegradable pots, such as toilet rolls or newspaper pots, you can put the whole pot straight into the ground.) Fill the hole with compost or soil, and firm it around the plant so it doesn't wobble. Give it a water and hey presto, you've replanted your seedling.

C. GROWING FROM SCRAPS

What if I told you that you could easily grow vegetables from kitchen trimmings, on a windowsill? I didn't believe it until I started growing spring onions (scallions) from roots in a glass of water. Overnight, they'd grown by 5 cm (2 in) – it was incredible to watch.

Growing from scraps is a great way of cutting down on food waste and growing food for free from very little. It works for leafy vegetables such as lettuce and pak choi, root vegetables including potatoes, alliums such as onions, garlic and leeks, and herbs. I give full details on each of these in the Let's Grow chapter (pages 78–169).

You can also grow vegetables from the seeds of shop-bought produce, such as tomatoes and butternut squash. Do bear in mind that some of them are bred in such a way that they won't thrive in domestic settings: I suggest using seeds from organic varieties as they tend to be more successful. Some plants, when grown at home from shop-bought veg like squashes and potatoes, can turn out to be toxic. It's taken years of breeding to get rid of the toxins that were naturally in them to start with and occasionally a rogue plant will return to form. It's usually easy to spot because the produce will taste bitter. If you find this, stop eating it. (Chill cookie, these cases are rare – it's just good to mention these things.)

A NOTE ON WEEDING

Weeds are not evil, they are simply plants that are in the wrong place. That could mean an invasive species, such as nettles or bindweed, or a seedling from another plant that simply isn't what you desire. Unfortunately, weeds are bad for the plants you are trying to grow. They take some of the nutrients your plants need, weakening the crop, while crowding the space which hampers air circulation and makes fungal infections more likely.

The amount of time you spend weeding depends on how much space you have, whether your veg patch is in containers or in the soil and whether you have gone down the no-dig route. Either way, if you keep on top of weeding, you'll prevent it becoming a big task that will take days to complete. So as soon as you clap eyes on a weed, remove it fully, including the root, with a hand fork or trowel. Throw weeds onto the compost heap (if they aren't carrying flowers or seeds) or into the bin (if they are).

3.
YOUR SPACE

Whatever your space, no matter how big or small, the key is to be positive and creative with it. I've lived in an array of places over the years, from a high-rise flat to a shared house with a paved garden, and had an allotment (victory garden) and assisted at a local community garden. During all of this, I've been able to grow vegetables by being imaginative with the space I've had, and I've also managed to keep the costs down by being thrifty, speaking to other gardeners and watching a lot of online tutorials. There are perks to having a small space: the smaller it is, the less tending and watering is required.

The first thing you want to do before setting up your vegetable patch is to assess what you're working with:

SPACE: from an initial glance, you might think that you'll only be able to fit in a couple of containers. But have a proper look around and assess the walls – remember you can grow things vertically. Even if you don't have much indoor space, do you have any ledges, alleyways or space outside your front door to put a few containers? Could you put up hanging baskets anywhere? Get creative: where there's a will, there's a way. Also determine whether you can fit a compost bin outside or inside.

WATER: this one is a biggie as without water, we won't have any vegetables. Determine how you can gather rainwater and sort out a bucket for grey water (page 34). If you're going to need to use mains water, determine whether you're on a fixed rate or on a meter – in which case, you may find yourself with a very big water bill and some angry housemates/parents.

LIGHT AND WIND: observe your space for a few days and you'll see where the sun rises and sets as well as where the light hits your space at certain times during the day. Most vegetables tend to do alright with 4 hours of sunlight a day. Plants such as herbs and salad leaves are more forgiving, but plants that produce fruit will need plenty of sun because they're working harder to produce the goods. If your vegetable patch is on a balcony or a roof terrace, you might need to provide some shelter to protect your produce from the wind.

GROUND: containers work a treat indoors, on balconies, paved areas and roof terraces while raised beds or planting straight into the ground are what you want in larger outside spaces.

WHAT IF I DON'T HAVE ANY SPACE AT ALL?

You might live in a property which simply doesn't have any space to host a vegetable patch (though you really can grow a few veggies on your windowsill, on a shelf in the bathroom or on a table by the window – see pages 66–67). This is where allotments and community gardens come in:

ALLOTMENT (VICTORY GARDEN): this is a plot of land that you can hire for an annual fee, which includes provision of water. You are expected to look after your plot, and if you don't you can be booted off. Allotments are a big commitment, so do bear that in mind when signing up for one. If you definitely do want one, put your name down asap as waiting lists tend to be quite long.

COMMUNITY GARDEN: this is a plot of land that is looked after by a group of people. These gardens are incredibly popular in big cities worldwide, with over 550 of them in New York and 100 in London. Taiwan is another hotspot, where areas unsuitable for urban development are turned into gardens, and so is Spain, where a lot of younger people move to the cities from the countryside for work. Community gardens play a role in supplying produce to local residents and volunteers as well as providing vital space where people can develop a healthier, more sustainable food culture. Join a community garden and not only will you get vegetables out of it, you will also find yourself with a new bunch of friends and might even learn about cultures from around the world.

Guerilla gardening

This is when gardeners grow produce on land that they don't have legal rights to, such as abandoned sites or private property, as an act of political protest. It's often done as a way to prove to authorities that the urban spaces we live in could be greener and that housing developments are having an impact on our environment as well as our wellbeing. The downside of this type of gardening, apart from potentially leading to a brush with the law, is that the vegetable patch can be destroyed by the authorities if they choose.

1. INDOORS

In the UK, one in eight properties don't have any outdoor space. This is so depressing that I try not to think about it too often. The lack of outside spaces is often a class issue and tends to be linked to income. Many simply cannot afford the higher rents that a garden space can command. However, if this is your situation, it doesn't mean that a vegetable patch isn't within your reach. Far from it.

You can successfully grow vegetables – including most of the vegetables in this book (see the 'What to grow where' chart on pages 80–81) – indoors. They can still thrive and you won't even have to step outside to harvest them. It does depend on how much space you have and how much of it you want to dedicate to growing vegetables: you may want to go the whole hog and get an indoor greenhouse, you might be ok with container-growing in your house, or you might just want a few pots on your windowsill, or a ledge in your bathroom. Be realistic, but there are options open to all of us.

Vegetables growing indoors are protected from the elements, you're more in control of their environment, and they improve the air quality around you as they soak up carbon dioxide and produce oxygen (plants are too clever for their own good sometimes). Do make sure you open the windows when you can though, to get the air circulating. This will help prevent mould growth on your plants (if plants do start to show mould, sprinkle a little cinnamon over them and it will sort it right out).

If growing vegetables by a window, be wary of the sun coming through it because it can fry your plants. Plants grown by a window can also become crooked as they lean towards the light, so turn them around regularly. Strong sunlight can also encourage soft, sappy growth and 'bolting', meaning that the plants spurt up instead of taking their time to grow, and will be weaker as a result.

WHAT YOU MIGHT NEED

SEED TRAYS: you can buy trays – though check that they're eco-friendly and re-usable so you can use them time and time again – or you can create your own from leftover containers (pages 48–50). Make sure you make holes in the bottom for drainage. You'll need to put something underneath them to contain excess water: try a plastic tray or even an old roasting dish.

PROPAGATORS: cover your seed trays with a 'roof' or a clear plastic bag to create mini greenhouses. This increases the temperature, helping to ensure that your seeds will germinate and thrive. You can make a DIY propagator from household items (page 57).

GROW LIGHT: you can't control how much light comes into your house and some plants need consistent light to thrive. This is where grow lights come in. These are simply lamps that provide the necessary light and heat for your plants. You can pick them up rather cheaply and there are many sizes and styles available so choose one that is suitable for your set-up.

SHELVES: a rack of shelves or a bookcase is a great way to get more plants on the go.

CONTAINERS: consider the size of these. The smaller the container, the more often you will need to water it. But it's easy to overwater larger containers sometimes.

INDOOR GREENHOUSE: you will need a little more space to accommodate this. Small ones are available or you could go all out and buy one with sensors that let you know when plants need to be watered or are ready to harvest. The latter are too high-tech for my liking and very expensive, though over time the prices will probably go down – and who knows, they might become the norm in kitchens across the globe in years to come.

2. WINDOW LEDGES, BALCONIES AND ROOF TERRACES

Even though you may live many storeys above the ground, you can still grow your own vegetables. Urban gardeners are often the most ingenious and I love spotting little pockets of green high up in the sky in cities. Temperatures tends to be warmer in built-up environments due to buildings retaining heat, and this works in your favour.

If you have a balcony or roof terrace, you might be tempted to completely fill it with plants. But you could find yourself overwhelmed with the amount of work you'll have to do caring for them. If you can, reserve a little spot for a chair and table so you can really enjoy this outside space, as a refuge from city life.

Before you start creating your own paradise, there are a few things to bear in mind:

RULES: if you're renting, check that your landlord and the council are OK with you growing vegetables on your window ledge, balcony or roof terrace. (And if you share that space with other residents, check with them too of course.) It shouldn't be an issue but we all know that authorities can have the most ludicrous rules sometimes, and the thought of you being ordered to remove your patch pains me.

WEIGHT: find out how much weight the window ledge or balcony can safely hold. I don't want anybody going down for murder because they piled too many terracotta pots full of compost into their patch and it collapsed and crushed someone. In fact, try and avoid terracotta pots if you can, as they're heavier than metal and wooden alternatives, plus you'll have to lug them up to your space. Position heavier pots close to walls and supporting joists.

WATER RUN-OFF: I was once on a friend's balcony as she was watering her plants, only to hear the neighbour who was sunbathing below start screaming as the water overflowed on to her. The sound haunts me to this day; please put trays or dishes under your containers to prevent a similar situation.

HOW TO MAKE THE MOST
OF YOUR SPACE

WIND AND SHADE: it can get windy up in these spaces, so if yours isn't that well protected, get yourself some netting or a reed screen to act as a windbreak. You can also create a natural one with plants like bamboo that will protect your veggies.

LIGHT: you may have lots of light or you may have lots of shade. Thankfully you can pick vegetables that thrive in either, as you'll see in the 'What to grow where chart' (pages 80–81).

YIELD: depending on the size of your space, I would suggest going for high-yield crops that maximise your harvest. Tomatoes, cucumbers, herbs and salad leaves are a good bet.

INTERCROPPING: this involves growing fast- and slow-cropping plants together. Fast ones will be ready to harvest before the slow ones have matured enough to need all the space. It means you don't have to wait to sow one crop at a time and you can optimise your space.

CONTAINERS: growing vegetables in a container is a doddle on ledges, balconies and terraces. You can grow in pretty much anything as long as it's big enough for your plant and has drainage (see my notes on the weight of pots on the previous page).

VERTICAL GARDENING:

when it comes to balconies and roof terraces, it's easy to focus on the area of the floor and forget that there's so much you can do with vertical space. Climbers such as beans or cucumbers can be trained to grow upwards on twigs, a trellis or even a ladder. You can get wall grow bags – including lightweight felt ones – hanging baskets that can be bolted onto a wall or hung off a rail, and of course you can use shelves. You can even create your own living wall by repurposing a pallet.

How to make a living wall

Whether you're short on space on your balcony or want to free up more space in your garden for furniture, upcycling a pallet is a brilliant way to create a vertical planter. It's also cheap and easy – two words that are music to my ears.

Only use a pallet made from timber that hasn't been treated with chemicals. You can determine this by looking for an IPCC (International Plant Protection Convention) logo on the wood. If it's marked DB (de-barked), HT (heat-treated) or KD (kiln-dried) then it's safe to use, but if it's marked MB (methyl bromide) then steer clear as it could leach toxins into the soil and affect your plants.

You will need
- 1 pallet
- Weed membrane (organic)
- Scissors
- Staple gun (or hammer and nail)
- Ready-made compost
- Plants of your choice

1. Lay the pallet down so that the side with the largest openings (usually the back of the pallet) faces upwards.

2. Use scissors to cut the weed membrane to fit the back and base of the pallet. Pull the material taut over the back of the pallet and staple it every 10 cm (4 in) around the edge as well as on the slats in the middle.

3. Turn the pallet over and place upright. Measure the length and depth of the vertical supports on either side of the pallet. Create pockets from weed membrane to fit either side of the vertical supports. Staple them into place to secure them.

4. Fill the pockets with compost and add your plants. I would suggest a mix of salad leaves, herbs and bush and dwarf varieties of fruit-producing plants. Once you've planted your veggies, water them and they'll be well on their way.

3. PAVED AREAS AND BIGGER SPACES

You may have a scraggy old paved area, such as patio, that is more accustomed to cigarette butts than it is to plants, or you might have soil. Either way, before you start planning your space, use the four rules on pages 63–64 to assess what you're working with.

A. DESIGN

Growing on a larger area of ground means you have space to play with and you don't have to worry about the weight of any containers you want to use, so you can really mix things up, playing with different textures and heights. However, don't go mad to start with unless you want to find yourself having a breakdown among your plants, exhausted from your watering regime. Divide your space into sections and slowly build on them over the seasons. Think about what you use the space for too. If you regularly host friends or family, perhaps you'd like to keep a part of it vegetable free? Do you want a table and chairs out there? If your place is rented then you're not going to want to spend a small fortune doing it up – but a lick of paint and some upcycled furniture can go a long way, as can a string of fairy lights.

If you're growing your plants in soil, mentally prepare yourself for more pests and potentially more weeding – though you can also explore a no-dig garden (pages 30–31). If you have an allotment, you can look into picking up a second-hand green house and a shed.

B. RAISED BEDS

I'm a huge fan of raised beds. They require a little more effort and investment than pots and containers, but they also need less watering, saving you time and money. Ready-made ones are expensive so I'd suggest making your own out of re-purposed materials such as pallets, spare timber, bricks or large tyres. One thing to remember is that you need to be able to reach the middle of the bed without stepping on the compost or any of your precious produce. You can make your beds unique by painting them, and they'll last for years. To fill them, use a mix of topsoil (the top layer of soil that is packed full of nutrients and organic matter) and ready-made compost so the growing environment is as rich as possible.

4.
LET'S
GROW

You've decided what you're going to grow, you've sorted out your space and you're raring to go. It's now time to dive in and start putting the theory into practise so you can reap the rewards of growing your own vegetables: the best part of having your own vegetable patch. Overleaf there's a handy chart which will tell you where each vegetable project in this book grows best, whatever your space.

For each vegetable in this chapter, there's a key so you can quickly cast your eye over it and determine whether it's one for you or not:

START: this indicates the best season to get the seeds going for this vegetable.

PLANT: when to plant the vegetable out into a larger container or space, be it indoors or outdoors.

SEED SPACING AND PLANT SPACING: how deep you'll need to sow the seed and how far apart you'll need to space the seedlings when you plant them out. This will vary with each variety, so please check the instructions before doing so rather than tagging me in an angry tweet when it goes wrong. Don't say I didn't warn you.

HARVEST: how long it will take your bountiful crop to grow and when to harvest it. It's always good to know this so you can plan ahead and anticipate when the goods are coming.

WHAT TO GROW WHERE CHART:	Indoors	Window ledges and sills	Paved areas
Salad leaves	✓	✓	✓
Herbs	✓	✓	✓
Tomatoes	✓	✓	✓
(Bell) peppers	✓	✓	✓
Chillies	✓	✓	✓
Pak choi	✓	✓	✓
Chard	✓	✓	✓
Beans	✓	✓	✓
Peas	✓	✓	✓
Cucumber	✓	✓	✓
Courgette (zucchini)			✓
Squash			✓
Garlic	✓	✓	✓
Spring onion (scallion)	✓	✓	✓
Onion	✓	✓	✓
Leek	✓	✓	✓
Radishes	✓	✓	✓
Beetroot (beet)	✓	✓	✓
Carrot	✓	✓	✓
Potatoes	✓	✓	✓

Balconies and roof terraces	Garden and allotment	Notes
✓	✓	
✓	✓	
✓	✓	If growing inside or in hanging baskets, try bush varieties.
✓	✓	
✓	✓	
✓	✓	
✓	✓	For smaller spaces, grow dwarf or bush varieties that need little space.
✓	✓	For smaller spaces, grow dwarf or bush varieties that need little space.
✓	✓	Grow vertically so don't need much ground space.
✓	✓	Indoors, grow snacking varieties such as Mini Munch. If you're short on space, train to grow up canes.
✓	✓	Take up a fair bit of space.
✓	✓	Take up a fair bit of space.
✓	✓	
✓	✓	
✓	✓	
✓	✓	Baby leeks and smaller varieties, such as Nipper, can be grown inside; larger varieties are best outdoors.
✓	✓	
✓	✓	
✓	✓	If you're tight on space, try smaller varieties such as Chantenay or harvest the carrots when they're babies.
✓	✓	

1. CUT-AND-COME-AGAIN SALAD

START:
All year round

SEED SPACING:
1 cm (½ in) deep,
1–2 cm (½–¾ in) apart

PLANT SPACING:
5 cm (2 in) apart or
15 plants per 30 cm
(12 in) container

HARVEST:
All year round
(4–6 weeks
to grow)

We all know what it's like to buy bagged salad from the shops only to have it turn soggy and inedible within a few days. With homegrown salad, be it indoors or outdoors, you will have crisp, fresh leaves on tap. And the best thing about it is that you can harvest the leaves from each plant and they will continue to grow, ready for cutting again in 2–3 weeks. You will be able to repeat this process up to four times, meaning you'll have leaves throughout the season, winter or summer.

You can grow a wide range of salad leaves: lettuce, spinach, radicchio, mizuna, rocket (arugula)... experiment!

Leaves that grow well together

- *Oriental leaves: rocket (arugula), mustards, mizuna and tatsoi*

- *Italian leaves: chicory, lettuce, rocket (arugula) and radicchio*

- *Everyday leaves: lettuce, watercress, spinach and chicory (endive)*

GETTING STARTED

Seeds

Seedlings for this kind of leaf aren't so readily available but that's not a problem because, trust me, they are a doddle to grow from seed. You can have a consistent crop throughout the year too, if you sow seeds every 2 weeks (not too many each time though: a packet of seeds can go a long way).

If you are growing indoors, use multi-purpose compost to fill a tray, 15 cm (6 in) deep, or an old crate with a few drainage holes punched in the base. Sow the seed according the instructions on the packet. As the seeds are small, you won't need to sow them very deeply. Keep them moist and you will be rewarded with seedlings within 1–2 weeks.

If you want a larger crop and have more space, sow the seeds directly outside during the summer. Sow in 'drills' – straight grooves made into the soil – which make it easy to distinguish young seedlings from weeds. For salad leaves, the drills only need to be 1–2 cm (½–¾ in) deep (though check the packet). Water the soil well, sow the seeds and cover with soil before giving them another watering.

TIME TO THRIVE

As your seedlings mature, keep the compost moist and water them regularly. They'll be very happy in a sunny spot and can also be grown in the same container as root vegetables that take longer to mature (intercropping – see page 73).

HARVEST TIME

Leaves spring up quickly: pick as and when you want to eat them – even the tiniest baby leaves are good to go. You can pick the leaves individually or you can harvest the whole plant – your patch, your rules. Harvest in the morning when the leaves will be at their most pert and juicy – a hard day's work of sitting in the sun can leave them slightly wilted.

Once you've harvested all the leaves of one plant, allow it 2–3 weeks to recuperate and grow back, giving it a little love in the form of homegrown or ready-made compost. You can harvest the leaves up to four times, after which they might start to taste bitter or the plants begin to flower. This is a sign they've had enough and it's time to let them retire to the compost bin.

Save your seed: leave a few of the plants to flower, if you can, and then wait for them to turn brown and dry out. Run your fingers along the stems and harvest the seed, ready for another crop whenever you want.

PESKY PESTS

- *Slugs*

HOW TO STORE

Leaves are best eaten fresh, but they will also keep in the fridge for a few days. If they're looking a little sad and wilted, you can pep them up by immersing in a bowl of cold water for half an hour or so.

How to build a salad

You can't really go wrong with a salad but there are a few steps you can take to make sure it's a knockout every time.

1. *Leaves*: pick the leaves you want to build your salad from.

2. *Extras*: every salad needs a little something special to give it character. This could be some roasted vegetables, or you might want to bulk up your salad up with a bit of protein – perhaps some halloumi or pan-fried tofu?

3. *Texture*: crunchy seeds, nuts, croutons or pomegranate seeds will elevate your salad to the next level.

4. *Freshness*: I adore handfuls of herbs mixed into a salad – they give real freshness and it's a great way of using whatever you've got laying around.

5. *Dressing*: a well-balanced dressing will make your salad sing. Use a two-to-one ratio of oil to acid (such as citrus juice or vinegar), and add seasoning to taste. Play around with different oils and acids to discover your ideal dressing.

2. HERBS

START:
Spring

SEED SPACING:
1–2 cm (½–¾ in)
deep and apart

PLANT SPACING:
15–30 cm (6–12 in)
apart or 4–8 plants
per 30 cm (12 in)
container

HARVEST:
Summer–winter
(4–16 weeks to grow)

I think we've all been the proud owners of a supermarket herb plant that has unceremoniously died even though it has been showered with love, affection and, probably, too much water. Well, there's no need to feel guilty anymore, or spend a fortune on herbs from the supermarket that go to waste because there's always too much in the packet (why is this?!). You can easily grow your own herbs and sit them somewhere so they're at your fingertips when you cook up another overly ambitious gourmet meal.

Combinations to grow together
- *Aromatic*: thyme, rosemary, basil and mint
- *Mixed herbs*: parsley, dill, coriander (cilantro), basil and chives
- *Perfect for cooking*: mint, chives, rosemary and perilla

GETTING STARTED

Seeds
Sprinkle seeds into a seed tray or into a container filled with ready-made compost before lightly covering with more compost and placing in a sunny spot. They should germinate within a week.

Seedlings

You can buy plants from the supermarket that you will be able to rescue by repotting and treating with a little love and care. Or you can buy plants from garden centres.

SCRAPS

With a single cutting, you can easily grow more herbs and it's potentially even easier than growing them from seed. It's best to use a healthy non-flowering cutting: a growing shoot, that's been cut in the morning to avoid wilting. Take a shoot 10–15 cm (4–6 in) long and strip the leaves from the bottom half of the stem. Put into a glass of water, ensuring no leaves are submerged, and place in a sunny spot. Watch the roots slowly emerge (don't forget to change the water every few days). Once the cuttings have roots, you can plant them into a compost-filled container, and water well, where they'll hopefully continue to thrive.

TIME TO THRIVE

Keep the compost nice and moist but don't overwater herbs that prefer hotter climates, such as rosemary, sage and basil. When you notice flowers emerging on your herbs, pick them off in order to encourage more flavoursome leafy growth. (Don't throw the flowers away – they make beautiful edible garnishes for both sweet and savoury dishes.) Leave a few flowers, though, to attract pollinators (pages 40–44).

HARVEST TIME

When you want to use the herbs, harvest from the top of the plant downwards, rather than going straight for the base of the stems – this will encourage them to grow back stronger and fuller.

PESKY PESTS

- Slugs and snails

HOW TO STORE

You can store cut herbs in the fridge, wrapping the stems in a damp cloth to prevent them drying out. If you fancy it, you can dry them by hanging them upside down in bunches in dark but warm space for 2–4 weeks. This works especially well with woodier herbs such as rosemary, thyme and sage. You can also dry them in your microwave by putting the leaves between two pieces of kitchen paper and microwaving on high for 1–2 minutes until dry and brittle. Watch them like a hawk as they have a tendency to burn very quickly.

For delicate herbs like chives and parsley, finely chop and pack into an ice cube tray before filling each hole up with water or olive oil, and freezing. You can also mix the chopped herbs into butter for a delicious herby butter that will store for up to a week in the fridge or a month in the freezer.

Salsa verde

Serves: 4
Prepare: 10 minutes

1 bunch parsley, approx.
30 g (1 oz)
1 bunch mint, approx.
30 g (1 oz)
1 bunch basil, approx.
30 g (1 oz)
2 tablespoons capers
(baby capers) or
chopped gherkins
(cornichons)
2 tablespoons red wine
vinegar
1 garlic cloves, crushed
100–120 ml (3½–
4 fl oz/½ cup) olive oil
sea salt and freshly ground
black pepper

This is exactly what it says on the tin – a green sauce, part of the same family as chimichurri and mint sauce. Salsa verde is nicely piquant and adds a delicious zing to all kinds of dishes, stir through scrambled egg, amp up a mega sandwich or slather over a breakfast hash. Play around with the herbs you use to create your own unique take on it.

1. Pick the leaves from the herbs, chop finely and put in a bowl. Chop the capers, if using, and add these too – or add the chopped gherkin. Add the vinegar and garlic.

2. Gently stir in the olive oil until you reach your desired consistency (you may not need it all). Season to taste. Serve straight away or store in the fridge for up to 3 days.

3. TOMATOES

START:
Spring

SEED SPACING:
1 cm (½ in) deep,
3 seeds per pot

PLANT SPACING:
30 cm (12 in) apart
or 1 plant per 30 cm
(12 in) container

HARVEST:
Summer (16–
18 weeks to grow)

The tomato is the king of vegetables (it's a fruit actually, but let's say vegetable for this book). It's also a great crop to start with if you're new to gardening as it's easy to grow and needs little maintenance. If you're tight on space, try smaller bush varieties that can be grown in a pot indoors – or use your outside space vertically with tumbling varieties that do well in hanging baskets. Either way, the smell of a tomato picked fresh from the vine cannot be beaten: it is simply divine.

GETTING STARTED

Seeds
Choose a small pot or a container about 10 cm (4 in) deep, such as an old yoghurt pot with drainage holes in the base. Fill to the top with multi-purpose compost and pop three seeds on the surface before covering with a thin layer of compost. Place in a sunny spot or use a propagator to germinate. When the seedlings are about 5 cm (2 in) tall, transfer to a larger pot of about 10 cm (4 in) diameter, to allow the roots to develop further.

Seedlings

Tomato seedlings are readily available in supermarkets and garden centres during the spring and early summer. As always, check whether they've been hardened off (page 58) and, if in doubt, harden them off yourself to be on the safe side.

If you want to grow tomatoes outside, wait until they're about 20 cm (8 in) tall before you put them out, and choose a sunny and sheltered spot. They will do well in grow bags, containers or in the ground spaced 30 cm (12 in) apart.

Scraps

You can grow new tomatoes from existing ones by scooping out the flesh from the centre of the fruit – see page 95. I would advise using organic tomatoes for this as they'll have been tampered with less and you'll have more chance of success.

TIME TO THRIVE

Water tomatoes regularly to ensure consistent growth and to avoid the fruit splitting (this can happen if you water them too much after a prolonged period of not watering them – or after a heavy downpour). None of this 'I can't be bothered to water my plants' tonight business.

If you're growing a cordon (climbing) tomato variety, you'll need to put a cane in the soil next to the plant to support it as it grows. This type of tom develops 'side shoots' – little shoots that grow between the main stem and the branches. Snap them off when you see them emerge or they will use up energy that you want your plant to put into making flowers and fruit. Ideally, you're aiming for each plant to have three or four branches so snap off the weaker ones.

Once you see fruit emerging, feed your tomato plants every 2 weeks with tomato feed.

HARVEST TIME

When the tomatoes are fully red (or orange, or yellow – or whatever colour they're supposed to be!), you can pick them. If you take any that are underripe by accident, put them on a sunny windowsill and they'll even out in a few days.

Save your seed: keep one of your tomatoes aside and scoop out the flesh. Put it in a sieve and run water through it until you're left with the seeds. Spread them out on a tray or some kitchen towel on a windowsill and leave them to dry out for a few days. Once they're dry store them in a glass jar in a cool dark place for up to 3 years.

PESKY PESTS

- *Aphids (greenfly)*

HOW TO STORE

Unless they're really over-ripe, it's best not to store tomatoes in the fridge as this can affect their flavour and texture. Cool room temperature is best.

Pa amb tomàquet

Serves: 4
Prepare: 5 minutes
Cook: 5 minutes

1 ciabatta loaf
1 garlic clove, halved
2 medium tomatoes,
    halved
extra virgin olive oil
sea salt

Note:
You can also grate the tomato flesh into a bowl and mix with olive oil and salt before spooning it over the grilled bread.

I grew up in Catalunya, where my life consisted of three things: sun, sea and pa amb tomàquet – one of the best culinary inventions of all time. A simple combination of great bread, great tomatoes and great olive oil, it's a glorious daily staple and integral to the Catalan identity. I think it trumps bread and butter any day of the week (haters gonna hate). The key is to use the best quality tomatoes possible, which is where the ones you've grown with your own fair hands come in. The olive oil is also very important: please use the best you can afford as it will elevate this simple dish to the next level. Eat pa amb tomàquet on its own or layer it up with anchovies, roasted vegetables or little cubes of tortilla for mini montaditos.

1. Preheat a grill (broiler). Cut the ciabatta in half lengthways. Toast the bread under the grill, cut side up, until just golden.

2. Rub the cut surfaces of the garlic clove over the toasted surface of the bread (don't skip this step – it's a deal breaker). Now rub the tomato halves, flesh side down, onto the bread, crushing the juice and flesh into the bread, until you are left with just the skins (discard these). Sprinkle over salt to taste then drizzle liberally with olive oil before cutting into wedges. *Bon profit*!

4. (BELL) PEPPERS

START:
Spring

SEED SPACING:
1 cm (½ in) deep,
1 per pot or 1 cm
(½ in) apart

PLANT SPACING:
40 cm (16 in) apart
or 1 plant per 30 cm
(12 in) container

HARVEST:
Summer–winter
(20–26 weeks
to grow)

I do love a versatile plant like this one.
The larger and less spicy brother of chillies,
peppers are a dream to grow indoors or
out – though they are sensitive to cold
weather. Grow them in a container or a pot
and, when the temperature drops over the
colder months, bring them inside at night.

GETTING STARTED

Seeds
Sow seeds in individual pots: they need to be
covered with just a light dusting of compost
and watered lightly. Place on a very sunny
windowsill or in a propagator as they like warm
conditions to really get going. If lack of light
is an issue, try a grow light (page 69). Peppers
take up to a month to germinate so be patient,
my friend.

Seedlings
Once the seeds have outgrown their first
pot (you'll know this when you see the roots
poking out of the bottom), it's time to move
them to a larger container or to their final
home. If you plan to move them outside you'll
need to harden them off (page 58) over a few
days so they don't die from shock –sounds
dramatic, but trust me.

Scraps

You can grow peppers from existing fruit.
Extract the seed and leave it to dry before
planting. As always, use organic varieties –
you'll have more success with them.

TIME TO THRIVE

Depending on the variety you're growing,
peppers may need a stick or cane for support
as the fruit can be quite weighty.

When you notice fruit emerging, start giving
the plant tomato feed every 2 weeks.

If you're growing indoors you'll need to
pollinate the flowers so that fruit can form.
Simply watering them from above is often
enough to spread the pollen from male to
female flowers, or you can use a paintbrush
to transfer pollen from one flower to another.
Be sure to have your windows open when
you can too, to encourage pollinating insects
to swing by.

HARVEST TIME

Your peppers are ready to pick when they've reached the right colour and are glossy in appearance.

Save your seed: remove the seeds from the peppers before you cook them and spread on a tray on a sunny windowsill to dry out for a few days. Store in a glass jar in a cool dark place for the following year.

PESKY PESTS

- *Aphids (greenfly)*
- *Slugs and snails*

HOW TO STORE

You can store your peppers in the fridge or keep them for longer by slicing them up and freezing them – or by preserving them with a recipe like the one overleaf.

Roasted peppers in oil

Oily roasted peppers are one of my favourite things in the world – the more oil, the better. As well as roasting, you can also sauté the peppers or char them on a gas stove (all hail the gas stove). I recommend using an olive oil that isn't overly strong or it will overpower the taste of the peppers. You can also add vinegar to this if you want a bit of a kick – I've included both options here. These gorgeous peppers go brilliantly on crusty bread, in an omelette, in salads, on a pizza or puréed into soup.

Makes: 1 x 500 ml
    (17 fl oz/2 cup) jar
Prepare: 5 minutes
Cook: 30 minutes

4 red (bell) peppers
1 whole garlic bulb
50–100 ml (1¾ fl oz–
    3½ fl oz/3–6
    tablespoons) olive oil
2 tablespoons red wine
    vinegar (optional)
sea salt and freshly ground
    black pepper

1. Preheat the oven to 200°C (180°C fan/ 400°F/gas 7). Put the whole peppers and the garlic bulb on an oven tray and roast for 20–30 minutes, turning the peppers halfway, until tender and charred. Alternatively, just roast the garlic but char the peppers over the flame on a gas stove or under the grill, turning them as they blacken.

2. Put the peppers in a bowl and cover with a cloth or put the bowl inside a paper bag. This makes it easier to remove the peppers' skin. Once cool enough to handle, peel off the skin and remove the stem and seeds. Cut the pepper flesh into long slices and separate the garlic cloves.

3. Combine 50 ml (3 tablespoons) olive oil with some salt and pepper – add the vinegar too if using. Put the roasted pepper slices into a clean 500 ml (17 fl oz/2 cup) jar along with the garlic before pouring in more oil so it comes to the top of the jar. If you don't have enough oil, top it up with a further 25–50 ml (2–3 tablespoons). Slide a knife down the inside of the jar to get rid of any air gaps. Seal the jar and store in the fridge. The peppers will keep for 3–4 months as long as they remain fully submerged in olive oil.

5. CHILLIES

START:
Winter–spring

SEED SPACING:
1 cm (½ in) deep,
2–3 seeds per pot
or 2 cm (¾ in) apart

PLANT SPACING:
30 cm (12 in) apart or
one plant per 20 cm
(8 in) container

HARVEST:
Summer–autumn
(fall)

Easy to grow on a windowsill or in a container, these beautiful fruits brighten up any space and will produce a crop year after year if you look after them. There are so many varieties, from tamer ones to those that will blow your head off – take your pick!

GETTING STARTED

Seeds
Plant 2–3 seeds about 1 cm (½ in) deep into a pot of compost. Leave them somewhere warm, such as a windowsill or near a radiator, until they germinate, which can take about a month. Once sprouted, keep them in a sunny spot to grow until the roots start coming out of the drainage holes.

Seedlings
When the seedlings are 10–20 cm (4–8 in) tall, it's time to transplant them to a larger container or into the ground.

TIME TO THRIVE

Chillies are quite self-sufficient, so watering them twice a week should suffice. Depending on the size of the variety you're growing, you might need to support the plant with a cane of some sort. They're very happy to share their space with herbs.

HARVEST TIME

Pick chillies when they're fully coloured and glossy – towards the end of the summer usually.

Save your seed: remove the seeds from a chilli and spread out on a tray on a sunny windowsill to dry for a few days. Store in a glass jar in a cool dark place for the following year.

PESKY PESTS

- *Aphids (greenfly)*

HOW TO STORE

You can store chillies in the fridge or you can preserve them for longer by drying them or by making a sauce like the one on page 104.

Speedy homemade chilli sauce

Makes: 1 x 450–500 ml (17 fl oz/2 cup) jar
Prepare: 5 minutes

2–5 fresh chillies, stalks removed
2 garlic cloves, crushed
1 onion, peeled and chopped
1 tin chopped tomatoes
2 tablespoons white wine vinegar
1 teaspoon sugar
sea salt

If you like a bit of spice then this chilli sauce will be right up your street. Try it with eggs, barbecue dishes or added to soups or noodles for an extra kick. The quantity of chillies will change depending on what variety you're using, so feel free to amend the quantity below depending on how much spice you can handle. Use the best tinned (canned) tomatoes you can – the better the quality, the better your sauce will be.

1. Put all the ingredients into a food processor and blitz until fully combined. Transfer to a clean 450–500 ml (17 fl oz/2 cup) jar and seal. The sauce will keep in the fridge for up to 3 days or in the freezer for up to 3 months.

6. PAK CHOI

START:
Spring–summer

SEED SPACING:
2 cm (¾ in) deep,
1 seed per module
or 2 cm (¾ in) apart

PLANT SPACING:
15–30 cm (6–12 in)
apart or 3 plants
per 30 cm (12 in)
container

HARVEST:
Summer (4–6 weeks
to grow)

Pak choi is great in containers – it grows quickly and doesn't need much room, which means you can pair it up with other plants to make the most of your space. It's a lovely vegetable to cook with, giving freshness to any dish it's added to.

GETTING STARTED

Seeds
Sow the seeds 2 cm (¾ in) deep in a seed tray and pop in a sunny spot. If you want to sow outside directly, do so in the early summer months, after the last frost of spring – they need some warmth to germinate. The wider you sow them apart, the more space the pak choi will have to grow and develop.

Seedlings
Plant out pak choi when the seedlings are 5 cm (2 in) tall and easy to handle. Make sure you firm them in well and water liberally.

Scraps
You can very easily grow pak choi from scraps. Cut off 5 cm (2 in) of the root and put it in a dish with water in a sunny spot. Within days, you will start to see new leaves sprouting. Leave it to grow for a few weeks and cut off the leaves as and when you need them.

TIME TO THRIVE

If it's in a very sunny spot, pak choi can be prone to 'bolting' – aka growing too fast – so position it somewhere with partial shade. Ensuring it is well-watered and keeping the compost moist will also help prevent bolting and result in lusher leaves.

HARVEST TIME

Pak choi tastes best when it's just picked so harvest as and when you need it. You can harvest the baby leaves for salads, when the plant is younger, or leave them to grow and use in dishes such as stir-fries.

PESKY PESTS

- *Flea beetle*

TO STORE

Store pak choi in the fridge wrapped in a damp cloth to prevent drying out. If it's looking a bit wilted, pep up the leaves by putting them into a bowl of cold water.

Garlic and ginger pak choi

Serves: 4
Prepare: 5 minutes
Cook: 5 minutes

2 heads pak choi, leaves
    separated
4 tablespoons vegetable
    oil
1 chilli, finely sliced
2 garlic cloves, crushed
2 cm (¾ in) piece root
    ginger, peeled and
    grated

Optional extras
soy sauce
sesame oil
sesame seeds

This recipe is inspired by My Neighbours, My Dumplings, a Vietnamese restaurant that I frequent with my good friend and fellow Cher aficionado Peter. Unless we have eaten this dish – along with the rest of the menu – we don't consider ourselves to have had a proper catch-up. At home you can serve it with crispy marinated tofu or fried mushrooms alongside coconut rice or vermicelli noodles.

1. Steam the pak choi in a steamer basket over a pan of simmering water for 2–3 minutes until just tender but retaining some crunch. Transfer to a warmed serving dish.

2. Heat the oil in a small pan over a medium–high heat. Add the chilli, garlic and ginger and fry for 30–60 seconds, stirring continuously so they don't catch and burn. Pour the hot, flavoured oil over the pak choi. If you like, you can drizzle over some soy sauce and/or sesame oil and finish with a sprinkling of sesame seeds.

7. CHARD

START:
Summer

SEED SPACING:
2 cm (¾ in) deep,
2–3 seeds per pot
or 10 cm (4 in) apart

PLANT SPACING:
20–30 cm (8–12 in)
apart or 6 plants
per 30 cm (12 in)
container

HARVEST:
Summer–autumn
(fall) (6–16 weeks
to grow)

An easy and versatile plant to grow
(much easier than spinach), chard's
glossy leaves and vibrant stems will add
colour to your patch whatever your space.
You can keep cutting leaves from the
same plants throughout the summer
and autumn – give it a whirl.

GETTING STARTED

Seeds
Sow two to three seeds into a seed tray or
directly into a container or the ground, 2 cm
(¾ in) deep. If you want a continuous crop,
sow seeds every 2 weeks.

Seedlings
When seedlings start to emerge, thin them
out so you're left with just the strongest ones.
When they're large enough to handle, you
can transplant them if necessary.

TIME TO THRIVE

Chard is happy in a sunny spot or a partially
shady one. If you're growing it indoors you
might need to use a grow light to keep them
happy during the colder months. If in a
sheltered spot outside, it will quieten down
over the colder months but will re-emerge
in the spring.

Water chard well to avoid the leaves turning bitter. It's a pretty hardy plant, though, and very forgiving if you do anything you shouldn't to it.

HARVEST TIME

You can pick the smaller leaves, at about 10 cm (4 in) long, for salads, or wait for them to reach maturity. Cut them at the base of the stem and they'll grow back again just like the cut-and-come-again salad on page 82. The more regularly you pick, the more you'll encourage chard to grow.

PESKY PESTS

- *Slugs*

HOW TO STORE

Store chard in the fridge with the stems wrapped in a damp cloth to stop drying out.

LET'S GROW

Sautéed chard with garlic and pumpkin seeds

Serves: 4
Prepare: 5 minutes
Cook: 10 minutes

800 g (1 lb 12 oz) chard
2 tablespoons olive oil
2 garlic cloves, crushed
1 lemon
2 tablespoons pumpkin
   seeds
sea salt and freshly
   ground black pepper

Chard doesn't seem to get much limelight compared to its cooler cousin kale, but (whispers in low voice) I think chard is a much better leaf. The recipe below is quick and makes a fantastic side for an array of dishes such as roasted cauliflower steaks, meat-free wellington or a nut roast. You can also turn chard into the most delicious bubbling gratin.

1. Separate the chard leaves from the stems. Slice the leaves into 2.5 cm (1 in) ribbons and finely slice the stems. Heat the olive oil in a large frying pan over a medium heat, then add the chard stems along with the garlic. Sauté for 4–5 minutes until the stems have started to soften.

2. Add the chard leaves to the pan, season and sauté for 3–5 minutes more, until tender.

3. Cut the lemon in half and squeeze the lemon juice over the chard, then add the pumpkin seeds and toss together. Serve straight away.

8. FRENCH BEANS

French beans are great for small spaces as you can either train them to climb upwards or choose a dwarf variety that will lay low and behave itself. They're also happy to share their space with other climbing plants such as squashes, wrapping themselves around the same cane together so you can grow more in less space.

GETTING STARTED

Seeds

Sow the seeds in a seed tray or a biodegradable container, one seed per pot about 5 cm (2 in) deep, and keep well watered in a sunny spot. You can also sow French beans directly outside towards the end of spring after the last frost, spacing them 15 cm (6 in) apart. If you're growing a climbing variety, plant them with a 1–2 m (40–80 in) cane so they can curl around it.

If you want to have a continuous supply of beans through the summer, sow seeds every 6 weeks though beware of growing too many – these plants are prolific, and you might find yourself with more beans than you know what to do with.

Seedlings

When they reach 10 cm (4 in) tall re-pot them and put them outside if you want to. Space them 20 cm (8 in) apart so they have room to spread. If you've gone for a climbing variety, add a cane and gently twine the plant around it to encourage it to grow vertically. Dwarf varieties don't need anything to support them and are lower-maintenance.

TIME TO THRIVE

As with most plants, French beans like the sun. If you're growing a climbing variety, make sure they're in a sheltered spot protected from the wind: they will grow to about 2 metres (80 in) tall if you're lucky and you don't want them whipping about in the breeze. Keep them well watered and, when they start to flower, give them tomato feed every 2 weeks to promote growth.

HARVEST TIME

Your beans are ready to pick when 8–10 cm (3–4 in) long. Harvest them regularly, using scissors for ease, as this will encourage the plant to produce more beans. If you can see the outline of the little beans in the pod, you've left it a bit late and the beans may be tough and stringy. If this is the case, you can de-string them and cut off the tougher parts before cooking the whole pods. However, you can also harvest and dry them for a few days inside and you'll have dried beans to cook with or seeds for next year – nifty.

Save your seed: if you want to save beans to plant next year, leave a few to fully mature on the plant and then dry the seeds in an airy place before storing them in a jar or an envelope in a cool dark place.

PESKY PESTS

- *Aphids (greenfly)*
- *Slugs and snails*

HOW TO STORE

French beans are best stored in the fridge where they remain crisp. If you find yourself with a glut on your hands, you can blanch them – cook very briefly in boiling water – before draining well and freezing them to enjoy throughout the colder months. You can also preserve them in olive oil or vinegar and water as well as turning them into a piccalilli-style preserve or a chutney with other vegetables such as cauliflower and shallots.

Lemon and garlic French beans

Serves: 4
Prepare: 5 minutes
Cook: 5 minutes

300 g (10½ oz) French
   beans, trimmed
grated zest of 1 lemon
   plus half its juice
2 garlic cloves, crushed
30 ml (1 fl oz/⅛ cup)
   olive oil
handful of parsley,
   roughly chopped
sea salt and freshly
   ground black pepper

Fresh French beans taste absolutely fantastic;
it's best not to mess with them too much if you
want to fully enjoy the flavour. You can blanch
them and serve them with a large chunk of
butter – always a winner – or combine them
with lemon and herbs as I have in this recipe.
Swap the lemon for orange or lime if you like,
and try different herbs as well.

1. Bring a saucepan of water to the boil and
    boil the beans for 2–4 minutes until they're
    just tender but retain a bit of crunch. Plunge
    them into a bowl of cold water for a minute or
    so before draining them.

2. Combine the lemon zest and juice, the garlic
    and olive oil and whisk together to make a
    dressing. Season to taste. Toss the dressing
    with the beans and add the parsley. Serve
    immediately.

9. PEAS

START:
Spring–summer

SEED SPACING:
5 cm (2 in) deep,
1 per pot or 5 cm
(2 in) apart

PLANT SPACING:
5 cm (2 in) apart
or 15–18 plants per
30 cm (12 in)
container

HARVEST:
Summer–autumn
(fall) (12 weeks to
grow)

Tomatoes taste epic eaten straight from the vine, but have you tried peas straight from the pod? It's possibly an even more life-changing experience – they are so good. Like beans, you can get climbing and dwarf varieties of peas, meaning you can pick whatever suits you and your patch best.

GETTING STARTED

Seeds

Peas like to be grown in a deep pot so their long tap root can stretch out: put one seed 5 cm (2 in) deep in a compost-filled toilet roll or newspaper pot to encourage this healthy root run. Pop them in a well-lit spot and keep them moist. They really do like the sun, so if you're not getting much light in, bring out the grow light (page 69).

Peas need some warmth to germinate but you can sow them directly outside in late spring when the weather has begun to warm up. Again, sow them 5 cm (2 in) deep and 5 cm (2 in) apart.

Seedlings

When 10–15 cm (4–6 in) tall, plant out peas in their forever home – making sure you harden them off beforehand if they're going outside (page 58). They need a sunny, sheltered spot – against a wall is a ideal, or you can stick a cane in with them or build a frame for them to climb up. If you're growing them indoors, make sure they're somewhere sunny so they can thrive. Peas won't compete with each other as other plants do, so you only need to space them about 5 cm (2 in) apart.

Scraps

Keep an eye out for bags of dried peas in the shops as you'll be able to use them to grow more peas. Plant them as you would the seeds.

TIME TO THRIVE

If you want a stellar crop of peas and you're growing them in the ground, work lots of homemade or ready-made compost into the soil beforehand and water well. Wherever you're growing them, they'll need watering regularly throughout their growing season – especially when they're flowering – to encourage growth. When the flowers start to appear, it's time to feed with tomato feed every 2 weeks to get the best out of the plant.

Pea plants create shade so you can plant radishes and salad leaves below them in the same container to maximise your space.

HARVEST TIME

As your peas are growing, you can pick off some of the shoots and add them to salads for a delicious bit of pea-flavoured freshness. The peas are ready when the pods are 6–10 cm (2–4 in) long.

Save your seeds: if you want to collect your own seed, leave a few pods on the plant until they dry and turn yellow before collecting the seeds from inside. Or you can remove the peas from the pods and leave them to dry on a sunny windowsill before storing them somewhere cool and dry.

PESKY PESTS

- *Birds*

HOW TO STORE

To retain their freshness, blanch peas quickly before freezing them for later.

Green pea dip

Serves: 4
Prepare: 5 minutes
Cook: 5 minutes

250 g (9 oz) peas (fresh
    or frozen)
handful of mint leaves
2 tablespoons olive oil
1 garlic clove, crushed
juice of ½ lemon and a
    little grated zest
sea salt and freshly
    ground black pepper

Optional extras
pinch of chilli flakes
50 g (2 oz) crumbled feta
    or grated Parmesan
2 tablespoons nuts
    (walnuts work well)

Really fresh little peas, in my opinion, are best eaten raw straight from the plant. If you do cook them, you'll only need to blanch them quickly before plunging them into icy water to retain their flavour and colour. However, if you have a glut of peas – especially slightly larger ones later in the season – try this delicious minty dip. You can customise this recipe by adding cheese or spices, or nuts for texture. It also works very well indeed slathered on sandwiches with other veggies.

1. If you're using frozen peas, pour boiling water over them and leave for a few minutes until they've defrosted before draining them. If you're using fresh peas, skip this step – you can use them raw. Either way, put the peas into a food processor.

2. Add the rest of the ingredients to the processor and blitz everything together to reach your desired consistency. You can loosen it with a little water if you like. Season to taste and it's ready to serve.

10. CUCUMBER

START:
Spring

SEED SPACING:
2 cm (¾ in) deep,
1 per pot

PLANT SPACING:
30 cm (12 in) apart
or 1 plant per
30 cm (12 in)
container

HARVEST:
Summer (7–
10 weeks to grow)

Cucumbers are a great vegetable to choose if you're a first-timer as they grow like billy-o. And once you've tasted a crisp, homegrown one you'll sneer at those in the shops. Some varieties of cucumber plant are quite big so, if you live in a smaller space, I suggest growing a snacking variety which will produce perfect mini cukes. You can also train them to climb up a stick or a cane, making the most of a smaller space such as a balcony.

GETTING STARTED

Seeds
It's best not to plant cucumber seeds before mid-spring as they need warmer temperatures to germinate. Choose pots about a palm-width wide and sow one seed per pot, 2 cm (¾ in) deep, then cover with soil and water them. Cucumbers don't like the cold so leave them to do their thing in a sunny spot such as a propagation tray or windowsill, and water them regularly so the compost remains moist.

Seedlings

Cucumber seedlings are available from garden centres from late spring to early summer. When buying them, check to see if they've been hardened off as you might have to do this yourself (page 58). Cucumbers don't like the frost so don't even think about putting them out until the final frost of spring has passed – you don't want to be known as the cucumber killer.

TIME TO THRIVE

Once your seedlings are 15–20 cm (6–8 in) high, or you've hardened off the seedlings you've bought, they're ready to go into the big outside world or into a larger pot. They'll thrive in a sunny yet sheltered spot. If you're putting them straight into the ground outside, enrich the soil first if possible with homemade or ready-made compost or manure. Cucumber plants have a habit of sprawling over the ground so, if you're tight on outside space, train them to climb up a trellis or wooden canes.

They will need regular watering around the base, to ensure the water goes down to the roots – and even more so when they're established and producing fruit. When you notice little cucumbers growing, start feeding the plant tomato feed every 2 weeks.

HARVEST TIME

When the cucumbers are the right size – depending on the variety you've gone for – cut them from the stem using a knife or scissors. Don't let them grow too big as the quality will decline. If it looks like you'll be getting a glut, harvest them when small so you can pickle them to create homemade gherkins (cornichons).

PESKY PESTS

- *Whitefly*: these little monsters thrive on cucumber plants, so if you spot them on the underside of the leaves, give them a good jet with some water to blast them off. If that doesn't work, put a few drops of washing up liquid (dishwashing liquid) and a squeeze of lemon juice into a spray bottle then top up with water before spraying the flies with it. You can also make sticky traps by smearing a piece of brightly coloured card with petroleum jelly and washing up liquid. Hang it up close to the plant and watch the whitefly flock to it to meet their sticky end.

- *Cucumber mosaic virus*: if the leaves of your cucumber plant are looking brittle and are different shades of yellow and green then you're in danger. Sadly, there's not much you can do except dig up the plant to prevent it infecting others.

- *Aphids (greenfly)*

- *Powdery mildew*

HOW TO STORE

Cucumbers are usually best eaten fresh but you can store them in the fridge for a few days. A good way of preserving them for longer is by pickling as in the recipe on the following page.

Pickled cucumber

Makes: 1 litre (34 fl oz/
 4 cup) jar
Prepare: 20 minutes,
 plus standing time
Cook: 5 minutes

2 medium cucumbers
2 tablespoons sea salt
200 g (7 oz) caster
 (superfine) sugar
400 ml (13 fl oz/1½ cups)
 white wine vinegar
1 teaspoon ground
 turmeric
2 bay leaves
1 tablespoon coriander
 seeds
1 teaspoon mustard
 seeds

There's nothing quite like a tangy pickle to really get the taste buds going. Pickling is an easy and economical way to preserve vegetables and the joy of it is you can play around with the spices you use. For a splash of colour, I highly recommend adding 1 teaspoon ground turmeric to your vinegar mix: it will turn your vegetables a gorgeous orange.

1. Cut the cucumbers into discs, half-moons or ribbons – whatever you prefer. Put in a colander and sprinkle over the salt. Mix with your hands, cover and leave for at least 2 hours, or overnight, so the salt draws out the excess moisture from the cucumbers. We want our pickles to be nice and crunchy, not soggy.

2. In the meantime, put the rest of the ingredients in a saucepan over a medium heat and heat until the sugar has dissolved. Leave to cool.

3. Rinse the cucumbers under running water to remove excess salt then put them into a sterilised 1 litre (34 fl oz/4 cup) capacity glass jar – or two 500ml (17 fl oz/2 cup) jars. Pour over the vinegar mixture making sure the cucumbers are fully covered. Screw on a lid and store in the fridge. The pickles will be ready in 3 days but the longer you leave them, the more the flavours will intensify. They will keep in the fridge for up to 3 months.

11. COURGETTES (ZUCCHINI)

START:
Spring

SEED SPACING:
2.5 cm (1 in) deep,
1 per pot

PLANT SPACING:
60–90 cm (24–36 in)
apart or 1 plant per
40 cm (16 in)
container

HARVEST:
Summer–autumn
(fall) (14–16 weeks
to grow)

Every summer without fail, you'll hear the words 'courgette glut' uttered by someone who's got their own vegetable patch. No one ever grows the perfect amount of courgettes: it's just the law. They are incredibly easy to grow, very productive and the plants take up a lot of space, so keep this in mind when you're sowing seeds or buying seedlings. You can eat the flowers, harvest the courgettes when they're babies, or let them mature a bit more – you get a lot of bang for your buck with these beauties.

GETTING STARTED

Seeds

As the plants will grow to quite a size, it's best to start them off in a little pot about the diameter of your palm. Fill the pot with compost, sow the seed about 2.5 cm (1 in) deep and cover lightly with more compost before watering. Pop them in a makeshift propagator (page 69) to help the seeds germinate.

You can also sow the seeds directly into the ground at the beginning of summer when things are beginning to warm up. Do this as above, spacing 60–90 cm (24–36 in) apart.

Due to the size of these plants, I would not recommend growing them indoors – though of course anything is possible if you're determined enough.

Seedlings

Courgette seedlings are readily available in shops during the spring months. When the seedlings are beginning to outgrow their pots (the roots will be peeking out of the bottom), it's time to harden them off for a couple of days (page 58) before planting them 60–90 cm (24–36 in) apart in the ground or one plant per (large) container.

TIME TO THRIVE

Courgettes like to be in a sunny or partially sunny spot and one thing that is non-negotiable for them is plenty of water. Use the cut-off plastic bottle watering technique (page 34) to ensure the roots get what they need. When you see fruit emerging on the plant, start giving it tomato feed every 2 weeks.

HARVEST TIME

If the courgettes grow too large they will become marrows – which is no bad thing though they have a creamier texture than courgettes and taste more bland. Courgettes have a habit of going from tiny to massive almost overnight so check the plant regularly. During the height of summer, you're going to have a lot of produce on your hands.

PESKY PESTS

- *Slugs and snails*
- *Powdery mildew*

HOW TO STORE

Courgettes are best eaten fresh though they will keep in the fridge for a few days. Baby courgettes are delicious preserved in a little olive oil for later on in the year.

Courgette frittata

Serves: 4
Prepare: 10 minutes
Cook: 20 minutes

400 g (14 oz) courgettes
    (zucchini)
about 3 tablespoons
    olive oil
4 eggs, beaten
handful of herb leaves
    such as mint, parsley,
    coriander (cilantro)
    and/or chives, roughly
    chopped
20 g (¾ oz) grated
    Parmesan (optional)
sea salt and freshly
    ground black pepper

Frittata is one of my go-to dishes. It's a great way of using all kinds of vegetables, in large quantities, as well as whatever herbs you have on hand. You can grate in the knobbly bits of cheese you've got lying around in the fridge too. Feel free to scale up these quantities.

1. Cut the courgettes into 1 cm (½ in) slices. Heat 2 tablespoons olive oil in a medium frying pan over a medium heat and fry the courgettes for 5–10 minutes until golden and tender. Transfer to a plate lined with kitchen paper and wipe the frying pan clean.

2. Mix the eggs and herbs together in a large bowl or jug and season. Add the Parmesan, if using, then stir in the fried courgette slices.

3. Heat 1 tablespoon of olive oil in the pan over a low heat and pour in the egg and courgette mixture. Fry for 5 minutes until the base and edges are set. Put a plate over the pan and flip the frittata onto it, then slide the frittata back into the pan on the other side. Cook for another 2–3 minutes until golden brown on the base. Serve with a green salad or pa amb tomàquet (page 96).

12. SQUASH

START:
Spring–summer

SEED SPACING:
3 cm (1 in) deep,
1 per pot

PLANT SPACING:
1 m (40 in) apart
or 1 plant per 50 cm
(20 in) container

HARVEST:
Summer–autumn
(fall) (18–20 weeks
to grow)

I've had varying degrees of success with squash as slugs have always managed to beat me to the harvest. I cannot describe the pain of turning over a butternut squash and seeing that it's been half eaten, it's like a dagger to the heart. Please learn from my mistakes: watch out for slugs like a hawk, they play dirty. See page 38 for earth–friendly ways to deter them.

You can get bushy squash plants or a trailing ones, depending on your space.

GETTING STARTED

Seeds

Sow 1 seed per pot 3 cm (1 in) deep and place somewhere sunny. If there's not much sun, use a propagator until the seeds germinate. When the seedlings have got 3–4 leaves they're good to go into a larger container or the ground.

Note: You can try growing from seeds saved from shop-bought squashes, but I have had varying degrees of success with them. Give it a whirl, but do plant some seeds you've bought too to avoid crushing disappointment. (And see my note on page 61 about potentially toxic squashes from saved seeds.)

Seedlings

Whether you've bought squash seedlings or grown them yourself, you will need to harden them off (page 58) and acclimatise them to the wider world if they're going to be moved outside. Don't even think about putting them outside until the last frost of spring has gone. Early summer is your best bet.

When planting them out into the ground, dig a couple of handfuls of ready-made or homemade compost into the soil before planting your seedlings 1 metre (40 in) apart. Firm around it and water well. If you've gone for a trailing variety of squash, put a sturdy cane in next to the plant so it can curl itself around it and grow upwards.

TIME TO THRIVE

These babies will need a lot of water during the summer months, so set up a direct-to-root watering system (page 34).

When you notice fruit growing, give the plants some tomato feed every 2 weeks.

HARVEST TIME

When your squash are ripe and a beautiful colour, it's time to harvest these beauties. Leave a short stalk attached at the top of the squash which will help prevent them rotting.

PESKY PESTS

- *Slugs and snails*

- *Powdery mildew:* if the leaves of your squash plant are covered in a dusty white powder then it's quite likely that they're suffering from a fungal disease known as powdery mildew. Remove the worst-affected parts of the plant and bag it up before binning it. You may want to spray the plant with on organic fungicide as well. You can prevent the disease in the first place by ensuring that the plants are well weeded to encourage air flow and planted in a sunny spot. Powdery mildew also affects cucumbers (page 119) and courgette (page 124).

HOW TO STORE

Put the harvested squash somewhere warm and leave them to ripen up for a further 1–2 weeks before eating. Alternatively, store in a cool dark place, where they'll last for a few months.

Smoky caramelised butternut squash

In case you haven't realised, I quite like saving time and cutting corners where I can. I'm a big fan of bunging everything into a roasting tin and letting the oven do the work for me while I squeeze in another episode of my latest Netflix obsession. This dish can be the star of the show with perhaps some lentils and leafy greens or it works brilliantly as a side with a nut roast.

Serves: 4
Prepare: 5 minutes
Cook: 45 minutes

450 g (1 lb) butternut squash, deseeded and cut into wedges (no need to peel)
4 garlic cloves, whole and unpeeled
4 tablespoons maple syrup or honey
2 tablespoons olive oil
1 tablespoon smoked paprika
sea salt and freshly ground black pepper
½ lemon

1. Preheat the oven to 200°C (180°C fan/400°F/Gas 7). Put the squash and garlic cloves into a roasting tin. Trickle over the maple syrup or honey and the oil, then scatter over the smoked paprika, salt and pepper and toss everything together so the squash is full coated. Roast in the oven for 45 minutes, stirring halfway through, until the squash is tender and caramelised.

2. Squeeze the roasted garlic out of the skins. Sprinkle the squash and garlic with salt and a drizzle more olive oil. Grate over the zest of the lemon half, squeeze over the juice and serve.

13. GARLIC

START:
Autumn (fall)–winter

SEED SPACING:
1 clove per pot

PLANT SPACING:
15–18 cm (6–8 in)
apart or 5 plants
per 30 cm (12 in)
container

HARVEST:
Summer (9 months
to grow)

Who doesn't like garlic? I mean how can you not? It's beautifully versatile in the kitchen and is happy enough to grow in a pot on a kitchen windowsill. It takes a while to grow but is no bother, so we'll let it off. There are two types: hardneck, which develops tall flowered spikes, and softneck, which doesn't and which has a longer shelf life. You can work out what type of garlic you have by opening up the bulb: hardneck garlic has a stem going through the middle of the bulb that hardens at maturity, with the cloves forming one ring around it, while softneck garlic doesn't have a central stem and has many cloves in a more random pattern.

GETTING STARTED

You can grow whole bulbs of garlic from single cloves that you already have in your kitchen. Is this witchcraft, I hear you cry? No, it's true. Break a garlic bulb into cloves and plant one clove per pot, pointy side up, with the tip up poking out of the soil. Water well, ensuring the pots can drain freely, and leave in a warm place to grow.

If you want to grow outside, plant the cloves straight into the ground or a container any time between autumn (fall) and spring depending on the variety you're growing (hardneck varieties prefer colder climates while softneck ones prefer warmer temperatures). Make sure the tip is facing up but submerge the cloves completely in the soil to prevent them being dislodged or targeted by the neighbour's cat when it decides to dig up your garden and use it as a loo.

TIME TO THRIVE

Garlic plants like to be in a sunny spot and will need regular watering while they're getting established. Once they're growing well, only water them if the soil has dried out – overwatering can cause the bulbs to rot. Keep an eye out for weeds and remove any as soon as you clap eyes on them as we want the plants to be well-ventilated.

HARVEST TIME

Patience is key with garlic. You'll have to wait a little while for them to grow but they make a lovely autumn (fall) treat when your summer harvest is over. Once the top part of the garlic stalk has turned yellow and basically looks like it's dying, it's time to ease up the bulbs with a fork or your hands. If you leave them too long in the ground the plant will start sprouting again and we don't want that.

PESKY PESTS

- *Leek rust*: if the garlic leaves are looking dull and shrivelled they might have leek rust, which eventually develops into orange pustules. Delightful. Thankfully, it won't make your crop inedible – the bulbs will still be ok. You can control it by spraying or watering the plants with a fungicide which will stop it spreading to other plants. Use an organic one so you can sleep easy at night knowing your crop isn't covered in toxic chemicals.

- *White rot:* if your garlic plants are yellow and stunted they might have white rot. Pull one of them up: if you see a white/grey mould on the base of the bulb, that's a sure sign. Dig up the affected plants and the surrounding soil to stop the rot spreading to any neighbouring plants and dispose of all of it. To paraphrase the immortal words of Ariana Grande: thank you but you're going in the bin. It can also affect leeks (page 147) and onions (page 145).

HOW TO STORE

Garlic cloves are at their sweetest and juiciest when freshly harvested. If you want to store whole garlic bulbs for a while, the plant will need to be completely dry. Lay out the freshly dug plants in a sunny spot for 2 weeks, until the skins become crisp. The n store them in a net bag, or with the stems plaited together into a rope, in a cool dark place for up 10 months (yes, 10!).

Roasted garlic oil

Makes: 340 ml (11¼ fl oz/
1⅓ cup) jar (a regular
British jam jar)
Prepare: 5 minutes
Cook: 40 minutes

3 whole garlic bulbs
100–150 ml (½ – ⅔ cup)
olive oil

Garlic is the love of my life. In fact, I'm very suspicious of people who say that they don't like it. It's delicious, tangy and the perfect people-deterrent. Hook it up to my veins please. This recipe promises a double garlic hit: not only do you get to enjoy the roasted garlic cloves – mashed into butter, spread on bread – the possibilities are endless – but you'll get a delicious and very versatile garlic-infused oil as well. The oil can be drizzled onto toasted bread, soups, noodles – whatever you want to add a garlic oil hit to.

1. Preheat your oven to 180°C (160°C fan/ 350°F/Gas 6). Slice the base off the garlic bulbs. Place them, cut side down, on a sheet of foil (this helps the cloves caramelise) then drizzle with some of the oil and wrap up into a foil parcel. Put in a roasting tin and roast in the oven for 40 minutes, or until the cloves are soft.

2. Once the garlic has cooled a little, squeeze the flesh out of the papery skins into a sterilised 350 ml (11¼ fl oz/1⅓ cup) jar. Pour over enough olive oil to cover the garlic, then screw the lid on. As long as the garlic is submerged in oil, it will last for up to a year in the fridge.

14. SPRING ONIONS (SCALLIONS)

START:
Any time except
autumn (fall)

SEED SPACING:
1 cm (½ in) deep,
1–2 cm (½–¾ in) apart

PLANT SPACING:
2 cm (¾ in) apart
or enough to fill
a container

HARVEST:
Spring–autumn (fall)
(8 weeks to grow)

The king of salad veg, spring onions are
incredibly easy to grow, whether from
seed, in a container or in the ground.
They're even easy to propagate from
kitchen scraps (page 60). What
are you waiting for?

GETTING STARTED

Seed
If you're planting in winter or early spring, get
spring onions going indoors in a seed tray or
in a container. Later on, you can sow them
directly into the ground or into a container
outside. If you're starting them off indoors, fill
your tray nearly to the top with multipurpose
compost, sprinkle over a few seeds and cover
with a light dusting of compost. Outside, sow
the seed thinly 1 cm (½ in) deep. They can
take a while to germinate so be patient. If they
are in a draughty spot, put a propagator roof
over them.

If you sow a new batch of spring onions every
few weeks, you'll have a steady supply from
spring until autumn (fall). You can even keep
them going all year round indoors if you're a
real spring onion addict.

Seedlings

Spring onion seedlings are readily available from online stores as well as gardening centres. Whether you've grown them from seed or have bought seedlings, when they're about 8 cm (3 in) tall they'll be ready to be moved outside into the ground or into a container and spaced 2 cm (¾ in) apart. Before you do this they will need thinning out, which means picking out the weaker seedlings so the stronger ones can thrive.

Scraps

Spring onions grow an absolute treat from scraps. Cut off about 5 cm (2 in) including the root and put it in a glass of water. Within hours you will see a new shoot emerging – it really is incredible. Over the space of a week or two, you'll find yourself with a new spring onion. You'll be able to grow them back from the same root three or four times. You can also plant the root in a container full of compost and it will thrive.

TIME TO THRIVE

These pretties are fairly low maintenance, as long as you keep them in a sunny spot and water and weed or mulch them well, maintaining plenty of air flow to prevent any mould on the leaves. If you do notice any mould, sprinkle some ground cinnamon over it and that should do the trick.

HARVEST TIME

When your spring onions are as thick as a pencil they're ready to eat. Harvest them as and when you want to use them as they don't keep very well. Just cut off what you need and the plant will grow back. You can, however, leave them in the ground and they'll grow into a larger onion.

PESKY PESTS

- *White rot*
- *Leek rust*

HOW TO STORE

Spring onions will store in the fridge for a few days. A top trick is to wrap a damp cloth around the roots to ensure they don't dry out and wither away.

Charred spring onions with salvitxada

Calçot is a large green relative of the spring onion common in Catalunya. It's so celebrated there that calçotadas – barbecues that celebrate this revered vegetable – are held every winter. The charred calçots are served with *salvitxada*, a nutty red sauce similar to romesco. This is a tribute to that dish, using spring onions roasted in the oven (thought you could also fry or griddle them). The traditional way to eat the onions is to peel off the charred outer leaves, dip the tender inner part into the sauce then tip your head back and lower it into your mouth. Baby leeks also work well in this recipe.

Serves: 4 as a starter
Prepare: 15 minutes
Cook: 1 hour 10 minutes

4 medium tomatoes
1 red (bell) pepper
5 garlic cloves, whole
    and unpeeled
100 ml (3½ fl oz/½ cup)
    extra virgin olive oil,
    plus extra for roasting
20 spring onions
    (scallions)
150 g (5 oz) flaked
    (slivered) almonds,
    toasted
1 slice stale bread or
    toast, torn into pieces
1 tablespoon red wine
    vinegar
sea salt and freshly
    ground black pepper

1. Preheat oven to 200°C (180°C fan/400°F/
   Gas 7). Score a cross into the base of each
   tomato (this will make it easier to peel
   them) and put onto a baking tray with the
   whole pepper and garlic cloves. Drizzle the
   vegetables with 1 tablespoon olive oil and
   roast for 30–40 minutes until tender. Leave
   to cool, then peel all of them.

2. Brush the spring onions with olive oil and
   put on a roasting tray. Roast in the oven for
   20–30 minutes, until charred.

3. Meanwhile, put the almonds and bread
   in a food processor and blitz to a coarse
   powder. Add the peeled roasted vegetables
   to the processor with the vinegar and two
   large pinches of salt then blitz into a paste.
   Slowly trickle in 100 ml (3½ fl oz/½ cup)
   olive oil while pulsing the processor, to form
   a thick sauce. Taste and add more vinegar
   if you wish (I tend to add more because I
   like the way it contrasts with the sweetness
   of the onions).

4. Peel back the charred leaves of the spring
   onions, dip it into the salvitxada, tip your
   head back and enjoy!

15. ONIONS

START:
Spring or autumn
(fall) for overwintering
varieties

SEED SPACING:
Sow 1 cm (½ in) deep,
2–3 per pot

PLANT SPACING:
15 cm (6 in) apart or
one to two plants
per 30 cm (12 in)
container

HARVEST:
Summer and
autumn (fall) (15–
20 weeks to grow)

Onions are one of the most used ingredients in our kitchens, forming the base of so many favourite dishes. I love them, even though they make me sob every time I use them (the only way I can stop this is by putting in my contact lenses). Good quality regular onions are cheaply and readily available in the shops, of course, so if you fancy growing some, turn your hand to more unusual varieties such as Egyptian walking onions, Italian Red Torpedo or Cipollini Yellow.

GETTING STARTED

Seeds
Pop 2–3 seeds, 1 cm (½ in) deep, into a pot about a palm-width in diameter. Cover lightly with compost before putting in a sunny spot. Water regularly and they should germinate within 21 days. When the onion shoots are 7–10 cm (3–4 in) tall, they're ready to plant out into a container or the ground.

Sets

'Sets' are mini onions that you put straight into a container or directly into the soil. They're readily available and are a very easy way of growing onions. Sets should be planted in spring. Onion seedlings are also available in the spring though there are fewer varieties to choose from than with seeds or sets.

Scraps

Onions are one of the gorgeous vegetables you can grow from kitchen scraps. Cut off the rooty base of an onion, remove any peel from it and pop it into a container with water. Check in on it every few days to note the root progress and change the water. Once you see roots emerging from the base of the onion, transfer to a pot of compost, ensuring that it fully covers the onion. After three to six months, you should have a mature onion.

TIME TO THRIVE

Like most plants, onions like to be in a sunny spot (don't we all?), so put them on a windowsill or somewhere indoors where the light comes in, or in your sunniest place outside. Make sure you regularly weed them – or mulch around them to suppress weeds. They hate competition and this will also minimise the risk of disease. Onions need regular watering as well; as soon as the surface of the soil is dry, give them a good glug of water. Watering regularly helps prevent onions from bolting – aka growing too quickly due to warmer weather. The water lowers the temperature of the soil, and stops the onions getting ahead of themselves.

If you've got a larger space or are part of a community garden, I'd suggest growing root vegetables such as onions, carrots and beetroot together. They like similar conditions and onions can also deter carrot fly, making them an excellent companion plant (page 37).

HARVEST TIME

Once the leaves start to droop and turn yellow, it's time to harvest your onions. Grasp the stalk with your hand and push a hand fork underneath the onion to lever it out.

PESKY PESTS

- ✏ *White rot*

HOW TO STORE

Onions are best stored in a cool, dark place where they will keep for a few months. But dry them out fully first, by leaving them in the sun or a warm place for a few days. This prevents mould forming – nobody deserves that to happen to them.

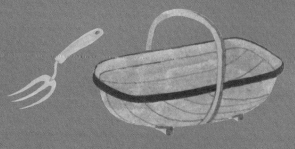

Quick pickled onion

Serves: 4 as an accompaniment
Prepare: 5 minutes

1 onion, peeled, halved and thinly sliced
1 tablespoon caster (superfine) sugar
juice of ½ lemon
large pinch of chilli flakes
large pinch of sea salt

I'm all for pickling produce in the traditional way but sometimes I want something that can add a bit of a zing to a dish within 5 minutes, and that's where these beauties come in. They go well in salads, on a dhal or in a sandwich. Red onions are great in this dish as they turn a vibrant purple colour, but it also works well with white onions.

1. Put all the ingredients into a bowl and combine well, giving them a good scrunch up with your hands. Leave for 5 minutes, until they've softened a little, then serve. They will keep in the fridge for up to 3 days.

16. LEEKS

START:
Spring

SEED SPACING:
1 cm (½ in) deep,
2 per module or pot

PLANT SPACING:
15–20 cm (6–8 in)
apart or 6 plants
per 30 cm (12 in)
container

HARVEST:
Autumn (fall)–spring
(25–40 weeks to
grow)

Leeks are great for beginner growers; they don't need the sun as much as other plants and are very happy doing their own thing in cooler temperatures.

In France, leeks are known as poor man's asparagus because they have a similar texture but are much cheaper and easier to grow. A lot of people seem to think that the green part of the leek should be thrown away because it's not as tender as the white part, but in fact it's packed full of flavour. Cook the green parts for a little longer to reduce the toughness and you shall be rewarded for your efforts.

GETTING STARTED

Seed
Sow the seeds 1 cm (½ in) deep in seed trays or toilet roll pots. They take 2–3 weeks to germinate, so be patient. When they are 20–30 cm (8–12 in) tall and roughly the thickness of a pencil, it's time to repot them.

Seedlings
These are readily available from your local gardening store. As with most seedlings, you should find out if they've been hardened off (page 58) before putting them into their new home – I'm not sure there's anything sadder then killing a batch of seedlings mere days after you've bought them.

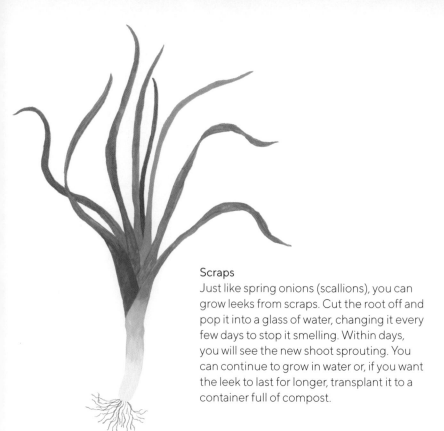

Scraps

Just like spring onions (scallions), you can grow leeks from scraps. Cut the root off and pop it into a glass of water, changing it every few days to stop it smelling. Within days, you will see the new shoot sprouting. You can continue to grow in water or, if you want the leek to last for longer, transplant it to a container full of compost.

TIME TO THRIVE

Leeks like a sunny spot but they'll also do well in partial shade so fear ye not. When it's time to move the seedlings to their new home, be it in a container or the ground, dig holes for them about 10 cm (4 in) deep and 15–20 cm (6–8 in) apart. Gently pop the seedings out of their pots – or, if you're using biodegradable ones (because you're a genius), skip that step.

Put the seedlings into the holes, fill the holes with water and then pat soil around the leeks so they're upright and stable.

Keep your leeks well watered in the summer months and that's it, you're golden.

HARVEST TIME

You can harvest baby leeks when they are about a thumb's width in diameter and they'll be sweet and delicious. Mature leeks are ready to harvest when the white part of the stem is about 10 cm (4 in) long. They're very forgiving, though, and will keep for longer in their container or in the ground, which is ideal as they're not great for storing.

PESKY PESTS

- *White rot*

HOW TO STORE

Leeks are best stored in the fridge. Wrap a damp cloth around the root end to stop them drying out too quickly.

Cheesy leeks with breadcrumb topping

Serves: 4
Prepare: 10 minutes
Cook: 40 minutes

3 leeks
70 g (2¼ oz) butter
1 garlic clove, crushed
2 slices bread, crusts
    removed, torn into
    pieces
50 g (2 oz) walnuts
leaves from 1 sprig thyme
leaves from 1 sprig
    rosemary
1 tablespoon olive oil
100 ml (3½ fl oz/½ cup)
    single (light) cream
50 g (2 oz) Cheddar,
    grated (shredded)
sea salt and freshly
    ground black pepper

This dish is the epitome of comfort food for me. It might have something to do with the amount of butter and cream that's involved – always a good thing in my book. Cooking the leeks for a decent amount of time makes them deliciously sweet and takes the dish to another level – it's worth the wait.

1. Wash the leeks then slice them into 1 cm (½ in) rounds. Melt the butter in an ovenproof, lidded frying pan over a medium heat, add the garlic for about a minute then add the leeks. Season then cover with a lid and leave to cook for 25-30 minutes, stirring occasionally, until very soft and sweet.

2. Meanwhile, make the breadcrumb topping by putting the bread, walnuts and herbs in a food processor and blitzing to crumbs. Mix in the olive oil to coat the crumbs and season.

3. Preheat your grill (broiler). Stir the cream and cheese into the leeks then sprinkle the breadcrumb mix over the top. Place the pan under the hot grill for 3-5 minutes, keeping an eye on it, until golden brown.

17. RADISHES

START:
Spring–autumn (fall)

SEED SPACING:
1–2 cm (½–¾ in) deep,
3 cm (1 in) apart

PLANT SPACING:
15 cm (6 in) apart or
as many as you can fit
into a container

HARVEST:
Summer–winter
(4–6 weeks to grow)

Fiery little radishes are some of the
quickest vegetables you can grow in
your patch and they don't take up much
space at all. They grow well with root
vegetables such as carrots: you can
harvest them before the larger veg
have reached full maturity.

GETTING STARTED

Seeds
To avoid a glut, sow radishes little and often.
You can start them in a tray or your trusty egg
carton, planting a seed in each hole, about
1 cm (½ in) deep. These are hardy plants and
germinate pretty easily: they'll do well on a
windowsill or a sunny spot outside, sharing a
space with other plants.

You can also sow them directly outside,
2 cm (¾ in) deep and 15 cm (6 in) apart. Winter
varieties need more room so space them
as per the instructions for the variety you're
working with.

Seedlings
As the seedings grow, thin them out, leaving
the strongest plants in the soil (yes, this is
survival of the fittest). They'll need hardening
off before you move them outside (page 58).

Scraps

Like other root vegetables, you can regrow radish leaves from scraps. Trim off the top of a radish and put it in a dish of water in a sunny spot, changing the water every couple of days. Within a week or two, more leaves will begin to emerge. You can leave it in the water or move it to a pot of compost where it will grow more quickly.

TIME TO THRIVE

As radishes grow so quickly, you can plant them in the same space as slower-growing root vegetables (intercropping – see page 73): they'll be harvested before the root vegetables have fully matured and need all the space. Water radishes well and regularly so they don't bolt or become woody, and weed around them to ensure they thrive.

HARVEST TIME

Radishes grow in the blink of an eye. You'll see the top of the root peeking out from the soil and that will give you an indication of how big it is. They taste best when they're young and tender, becoming spicier and woodier the longer you leave them in the ground.

PESKY PESTS

- ◢ *Slugs and snails*

HOW TO STORE

Radishes are best eaten fresh but you can also store them in the fridge wrapped in a damp cloth. Remove the leaves and store them separately or they will draw moisture out of the root. You can also slice the radishes and blanch them before freezing them or pickle them and use to add zing to many dishes.

Roasted radishes with sautéed radish tops

Serves: 4 as an accompaniment
Prepare: 5 minutes
Cook: 25 minutes

1 bunch radishes, roughly 400 g (14 oz), washed, leaves removed and set aside
2 tablespoons olive oil
1 garlic clove, crushed
sea salt and freshly ground black pepper

Roasting radishes is an absolute game changer; they become juicy and lose their spiciness, turning into sweet little bites of joy. The leafy tops are often overlooked but if you have some, do try sautéing them with garlic – they are a lovely accompaniment to the roasted radishes.

1. Preheat oven to 200°C (180°C fan/400°F/ Gas 7). Put the radishes into a roasting tray and drizzle with 1 tablespoon olive oil. Roast for 20 minutes until tender and golden.

2. Five minutes before your radishes are ready, heat 1 tablespoon of oil in a fryingpan and fry the crushed garlic for 30 seconds. Add the radish leaves and sauté for 2 minutes until wilted. Season to taste.

3. Season the roasted radishes and serve with the sautéed tops.

18. BEETROOTS (BEETS)

START:
Spring–summer

SEED SPACING:
2 cm (¾ in) deep,
1 per pot

PLANT SPACING:
10 cm (4 in) apart or
10 plants per 30 cm
(12 in) container

HARVEST:
Summer–autumn
(fall) (12–16 weeks
to grow)

I didn't eat beetroot for many years. This is because my Nan used to serve me awful over-boiled ones, the smell of which haunts me to this day. I somehow tasted them again at some point and since then I've become hooked – especially on growing them. They're easy and trouble-free, which means they're perfect for beginners.

GETTING STARTED

Seeds

Fill your seed trays or egg cartons with multi-purpose compost and sow one seed per pot 2 cm (¾ in) deep. Firm the compost and water well before putting in a sunny spot to germinate. They may benefit from a propagator if you're not getting a lot of light. The seedlings will need thinning out, so keep the stronger seedlings and throw the weaker ones into your compost bin or you can eat them as micro greens – they taste great in salads or in a sandwich.

Seedlings

Readily available from gardening centres, beetroot seedlings can be sown directly into the ground outside in late spring. Whether you've grown them yourself or have bought seedlings, when they're about 7.5 cm (3 in) tall, move them outside into the ground or into a container, 2 cm (¾ in) deep and spaced 10 cm (4 in) apart.

Scraps

Cut the top 2.5 cm (1 in) off a beetroot and pop it into a dish with water. The leaves will start to sprout and before you know it, you can harvest. If you want to get more leaves for longer, plant the top into a container of compost.

TIME TO THRIVE

The more space you give beetroot, the bigger they will grow, so plant further apart if you have the space. Naturally, if you give them less space, they'll be smaller but you'll have more of them! Do whatever tickles your fancy.

Keep the plants moist but avoid overwatering as this will encourage more leafy growth when we want the focus to be on the root.

Make sure you keep them well weeded or mulched so they don't have to compete for nutrients with weeds. Remember the prize here is the root, so no distractions because of the beautiful leaves please.

HARVEST TIME

Beetroot can be harvested once they reach the size of a golf ball, but you can leave them in the ground to get bigger, and even to grow on over winter.

PESKY PESTS

- *Birds*

TO STORE

The roots store pretty well in the fridge for quite a few weeks as long as you trim off the leaves first (please don't throw these away – you can sauté them like you would other leafy greens). Beetroot can also be packed in sawdust in a cool dark place for 2–3 months.

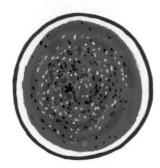

Beetroot hummus

I love beetroot's earthy flavour and it shines through in this hummus. You can boil the beetroot if you like (it will take 50 minutes–1 hour), but I prefer to roast them because it adds another level of flavour to the hummus. The beetroot peel can be turned into the most delicious crisps (chips): drizzle with olive oil and season before baking in the oven at 200°C (180°C fan/400°F/Gas 7) for 10–15 minutes until crisp – just make sure you scrub the outside really well.

Serves: 4 as a snack
or starter
Prepare: 10 minutes
Cook: 1 hour

3 beetroots (beets),
350–400 g (12–14 oz)
total
1 garlic clove, crushed
2 tablespoons tahini
juice of ½ lemon
4 tablespoons olive oil
sea salt and freshly ground
black pepper

Optional extras
mint leaves, roughly
chopped
1 tablespoon mixed seeds

1. Preheat oven to 200°C (180°C fan/400°F/Gas 7). Rub the beetroots with 1 tablespoon oil, put them in a roasting tin and season, then roast in the oven for 45 minutes–1 hour until tender. Leave the beetroots to cool before removing the skin.

2. Roughly chop the cooked beetroot and put in a food processor along with the garlic, tahini, lemon juice and remaining oil. Blitz the ingredients together until you've reached your desired consistency. Season to taste and serve, topping with the mint and mixed seeds if using. The hummus will keep in the fridge for 3 days or in the freezer for up to 3 months.

19. CARROTS

START:
Winter–summer

SEED SPACING:
1 cm (½ in) deep,
5–20 cm (2–8 in)
apart (depending
on variety)

PLANT SPACING:
5–20 cm (2–8 in)
apart (depending on
variety) or 35 plants
per 30 cm (12 in)
container

HARVEST:
Spring–autumn
(fall) (14–20 weeks
to grow)

My love affair with carrots began when I was told that if I ate them, I would be able to see in the dark. I was blind as a bat with coke-bottle glasses and desperate for this to be true, so I ate a lot of carrots. Nothing ever happened and I realised I'd been the victim of a cruel hoax. Thankfully I've managed to get over it. I still have poor vision and I still love carrots. They're pretty easy to grow as long as they have a deep enough space. If you're growing them inside, I'd suggest a smaller variety such as Chantenay.

GETTING STARTED

Seeds
Carrots are best sown direct into their final growing site. Sow in a container or into the ground in a partially shady spot. Make holes 1 cm (½ in) deep, 5–20 cm (2–8 in) apart – check the packet for instructions as planting distance varies a lot depending on the variety – the bigger the carrot, the bigger the space. Put one seed in each hole. Cover with compost and keep moist while the seeds germinate.

If you're growing them in the ground, dig in some ready-made or homemade compost or mulch the space beforehand to give the carrots nutrients. Make sure the ground is stone-free, which encourages the carrots to grow straight.

Seedlings

When seedlings start poking through, thin out the weaker ones. If you're using seedlings that you've acquired, find out whether they've been hardened off (page 58).

Also make sure that you've separated every seedling as they can be sold in clusters; if you plant them like that, things get a little cramped (understatement of the year). Space them out following the instructions for the variety you're working with.

Scraps

Cut off the top of a carrot and place it in a dish of water. Alternatively, leave the scrap to dry for a day, which will prevent it rotting then plant it into a pot of compost with only the top peeking out. Over 1–2 weeks, new green shoots will start to sprout. You can harvest them to make dishes such as pesto or, once roots have started sprouting at the base, repot them, so they keep sprouting for longer.

TIME TO THRIVE

Make sure carrots are well weeded. Water regularly, though don't overdo it as you don't want to encourage the leaves to grow too much at the expense of the root.

HARVEST TIME

The diameter of the carrot peeking out of the soil is a good indicator of how big the root is. You can pull them up earlier on in the year when they're babies or leave them to mature well into the winter. Baby and grown-up carrots are two completely different beasts with different flavours so you're getting two for the price of one really.

PESKY PESTS

- *Carrot fly*: these are crafty little blighters with very good carrot radar – they can literally smell the roots – and once they appear, there's not much you can do about them. You'll know you've got them if there are little brown scars around the carrot. If you see this, please don't eat the carrot: the flies can turn into maggots and the thought of accidentally eating one of them makes me retch. You can prevent carrot fly by minimising any disturbance around the growing root, and by thinning the seedlings or weeding in the evening when the flies are less active. Smart companion planting works too (page 37): go for alliums such as spring onions and chives that mask the carrot smell. You can also put a fine mesh net over your growing carrots.

HOW TO STORE

Carrots are happy to do their thing in the ground until you need them, though if you find yourself with a glut, you can store them for a few days in the fridge. Remove the leafy carrot tops and use them in green sauces. You can also blanch carrots and freeze them for a later date.

Roasted carrots
with carrot top chimichurri

I'm a big fan of root to shoot cooking, ensuring that as much of the vegetable as possible gets used. So much of our food goes to waste and discovering new ways to minimise that is all part of the fun of growing and cooking. Carrot tops are an incredibly versatile ingredient, often overlooked in my humble opinion, and they work beautifully in this zingy chimichurri sauce, an Argentinian speciality. I highly recommend giving carrot top pesto a whirl as well.

Serves: 4 as a side dish
Prepare: 15 minutes
Cook: 30 minutes

1 bunch carrots with tops, roughly 400 g (14 oz) total
150 ml (5 fl oz/⅔ cup) olive oil
large handful of parsley leaves, finely chopped
2 teaspoons dried oregano
large pinch of chilli flakes
2 garlic cloves, crushed
2 tablespoons red wine vinegar
sea salt and freshly ground black pepper

1. Preheat the oven to 200°C (180°C fan/ 400°F/Gas 7). Trim off the carrot tops and put to one side. Cut the carrots in half lengthwise and then half again so you have four long pieces. Put them into a roasting tin, drizzle with 2 tablespoons olive oil and season. Roast for 20– 30 minutes until tender.

2. Meanwhile, make the chimichurri. Give the carrot tops a good wash, then finely chop them. Put them in a bowl with the parsley, oregano, chilli flakes, garlic, vinegar and the remaining olive oil before giving everything a good mix. Season to taste. You might want to add more vinegar if you're obsessed with the stuff like I am.

3. Serve the hot roasted carrots with the chimichurri drizzled over the top. Any leftover sauce will last for up the three days in the fridge – you'll just need to stir in a little more olive oil to loosen it up.

20. POTATOES

START:
Spring–summer

SEED SPACING:
10 cm (4 in) deep,
30 cm (12 in) apart

HARVEST:
Summer–autumn
(fall) (12–16 weeks
to grow)

If Matt Damon can grow potatoes on Mars (in *The Martian*), then you can definitely grow potatoes in your space. Regular potatoes are easy and cheap to source locally, so if you're growing your own, try your hand at varieties that are more expensive to buy, such as Yukon Gold, Salad Blue and Purple Majesty.

GETTING STARTED

Seed potatoes

Seed potatoes are small spuds that will sprout and form a new plant. To get them ready for planting, you need to 'chit' them, which in layman's terms means allowing the eyes on the potatoes to sprout. Put the seed potatoes in an egg box with the end with the most eyes upwards. Leave them in a sunny spot for 2–3 weeks until the shoots are 2–3 cm (¾–1 in) long.

You can easily grow potatoes in a large sturdy carrier bag or a bin, indoors or outside, or a deep pot. Whatever you use, make sure it has drainage holes. Either way, fill your container at least half full with multi-purpose compost (or, if you can get your hands on some topsoil, use a 50/50 mix of that and compost). Press the potatoes gently into the compost, shoot side up, 30 cm (12 in) apart, before filling up the container with more compost, leaving a gap of 10 cm (4 in) below the rim of the pot, and watering well.

If you're putting potatoes straight into the ground, dig a trench 10 cm (4 in) deep and space the sprouting seed potatoes 30 cm (12 in) apart. Cover with soil, banking it up as this will support the stem when it emerges, and water well.

Scraps

You may see people online growing potatoes from scraps. This can work but I have had varying degrees of success as certain potatoes are treated with chemicals specifically designed to slow down sprouting (this extends shelf life). If you're going to grow potatoes from scraps, use organic ones as they'll be more successful. You will need to chit them and follow the steps above.

LET'S GROW

TIME TO THRIVE

Potatoes like a sunny or partially shady spot. Keep them well watered and weeded. When you notice shoots emerging above ground, cover them with fresh compost or soil: this will encourage the plant to grow more tubers (aka potatoes). You can repeat this once or twice more, at 2–3 week intervals if you wish. If you're growing your potatoes in a container, fill it to the top with compost.

Also, we don't want the potatoes to turn green, which happens when they are exposed to light. The green parts contain a toxin, and I really don't want to go down for accidentally poisoning someone or giving them a very bad case of the runs.

HARVEST TIME

When the plants start to flower and the leaves turn yellow, it's time to harvest – though you can harvest them beforehand if you'd like a few baby potatoes. If you're growing in the ground, dig them up with a fork; if you've grown them in a container, tip the contents out onto a sheet or tray and sift the potatoes out. Make sure you get all the potatoes, as any left behind could cause blight (see below). And if you're throwing the leaves into your compost bin, make sure the flowers have been removed or they'll start growing.

PESKY PESTS

- *Potato blight*: if you notice that the leaves of your plant are brown and shrivelled than you may have blight. It spreads quickly so as soon as you spot it, remove the affected leaves and bag them up for the green waste collection or burn them. If you catch it quick enough then your potatoes might be blight-free. Dig up a few and if the flesh inside isn't stained brown or rotting then you're safe. You can leave the potatoes in the ground and harvest them as usual.

HOW TO STORE

Once you've harvested your potatoes, dry them out for a few days in the sun so their skin 'cures' – they'll keep for longer. They like to be stored somewhere cool and dark, so the basement your landlord specifically told you not to use is a great shout. Don't store them in the fridge as the low temperature can turn the potato starch into sugar, making them taste unpleasant.

Spanish tortilla

Serves: 6
Prepare: 10 minutes
(plus optional 20 minutes
standing)
Cook: 40 minutes

500 g (1 lb 2 oz) potatoes,
    peeled
1 onion, peeled and halved
extra virgin olive oil, for
    frying
4 eggs
sea salt and freshly ground
    black pepper
handful of parsley, roughly
    chopped (optional)

A Spanish tortilla requires four simple ingredients which combine to create one of the finest dishes known to man. I was taught how to make it by a friend's grandmother and it's my all-time favourite comfort food. Growing up, I'd eat tortilla stuffed into a baguette which had been rubbed with tomato, olive oil and salt. I think it's best when the centre of the tortilla is still runny so don't overcook it. Serve it with pa amb tomàquet (page 96) and a fresh green salad. Scale the ingredients up or down, depending on how many potatoes you need to get through and how many people you're serving.

1. Slice the potatoes and onions about 5 mm (¼ in) thick – I would suggest using a mandoline if you have one (though please be careful – they're amazing but you also run the risk of losing a finger every time you even look at one).

2. Pour enough olive oil into a medium frying pan to cover the base by 2 cm (¾ in) and put over a low heat. Add the potatoes and onion along with a large pinch of salt and cook slowly for 20–30 minutes until the potatoes are just tender. If they go mushy, you've overcooked them but fear not – your tortilla will still taste epic. Meanwhile, whisk the eggs together in a large bowl and season.

3. Remove the cooked potatoes and onions from the pan with a slotted spoon. Fold them into the beaten egg until well combined. Season. If you've got time, leave the mix to rest for 10–20 minutes as this will help it thicken and allow the flavours to infuse.

4. Drain the oil out of the frying pan. Return 2 tablespoons of it to the pan and put over a medium heat. (You can use the rest of the oil for another recipe to avoid it going to waste.) Pour in the potato and egg mixture and cook for 5 minutes or until the edges are firm.

5. Cover the pan with a plate and flip it over so the tortilla comes out onto the plate. This takes practise and the egg will be a tad runny so do it over the sink. Slide the tortilla back into the pan the other way up and poke down around the edges to created a rounded edge. Cook for a further 2–3 minutes until golden brown. Slide on to a plate, sprinkle with sea salt and parsley, if using, and eat warm. Heaven.

FURTHER RESOURCES

There's a wealth of information out there for urban gardeners: online (where there's a video for just about every predicament or project you can think of), in books and through talking to other gardeners. The following are good starting points if you want to learn more and grow your skills.

INSTAGRAM ACCOUNTS

From stories on how to make the most of your space to envy-inducing photos from all over the world, Instagram's the place to go if you're looking for some online gardening inspiration and quick tips:

@66squarefeet: foraging and growing on a 66 square foot balcony in New York.

@blackgirlswithgardens: multicultural resource for those across the globe creating green spaces, as well as providing representation and inspiration.

@twodirtyboys: two friends running an allotment together in east London.

@bigcitygardener: urban gardener Timothy Hammond wants to make gardening accessible for everyone, especially in big cities.

@charles_dowding: the king of no-dig gardening – if you have any queries, his videos should be your first port of call.

@huwsgarden: Huw set himself the challenge of becoming self-sufficient by growing his own fruit and vegetables for a year. He succeeded and is now keen to show us how to do so too.

BOOKS

While you can source so much material online, you can't beat sitting down with a book. I've particularly enjoyed these ones over recent years and I turn to them time and time again for advice:

RHS Step-by-Step Veg Patch by Lucy Chamberlain

The Garden Jungle: or Gardening to Save the Planet by Dave Goulson

Planting for Honeybees by
Sarah Wyndham Lewis

Field Guide to Urban Gardening
by Kevin Espiritu

FREECYCLING

Save money and exchange goods
or pick them up for free from
people in your local area. Facebook
Marketplace and Gumtree (UK
only) are great resources for this
as are the following websites:

The Freecycle Network:
freecycle.org

Freegle: ilovefreegle.org

Recyclenow: recyclenow.com

ONLINE SEED AND PLANT SWAPS

Exchange seeds with other
gardeners from all over the world
or locate a plant swap a little bit
closer to home:

SEEDS
Seed Savers Exchange:
exchange.seedsavers.org

Seedswap: seedswap.org.uk

Seedsavers: seedsavers.net

Seeds of Diversity: seeds.ca

PLANTS
PlantSwap: plantswap.uk,
plantswap.com.au, plantswap.org

Crop Swap Australia:
cropswap.sydney

Eventbrite for ticketed events:
eventbrite.com

COMMUNITY GARDENS AND ALLOTMENTS

If you don't have your own space
or you just want to meet other
gardeners and help out in your
local community, these links are
a great starting point:

COMMUNITY GARDENS
Social Farms and Gardens (UK):
farmgarden.org.uk

GreenThumb (New York City):
greenthumb.nycgovparks.org

Community Gardens Australia:
communitygarden.org.au

ALLOTMENTS
Office International du Coin de
Terre et des Jardins Familiaux:
jardins-familiaux.org

Apply for an allotment (UK):
gov.uk/apply-allotment

Lend and Tend (Australia).
lendandtend.com

INDEX

Recipes are in *italics*

allotments 43, 64, 171
almonds: *Charred Spring Onions with Salvitxada* 140–1
animals 38, 40, 133
aphids 36

balconies & roof terraces 42, 70–5
    vertical gardening 74–5
barriers & deterrents 38
basil 37
bathtubs 51
bees 40
beetroots 154–8
    Beetroot Hummus 158
birds 38, 43
bolting 69, 106, 144
books 170–1
boxes 51
bricks 51
buckets 51
butternut squash. *see* squashes

calçots: *Charred Spring Onions with Salvitxada* 140–1
carbon footprint 11–12
carrier bags 50
carrot fly 144, 161–2
carrots 159–63
    Roasted Carrots with Carrot Top Chimichurri 163
cats 38, 133
CDs 38
chard 108–10
    Sautéed Chard with Garlic and Pumpkin Seeds 110
Charred Spring Onions with Salvitxada 140–1

Cheesy Leeks with Breadcrumb Topping 150
chemicals 36
chillies 102–4
    Speedy Homemade Chilli Sauce 104
chimichurri: *Roasted Carrots with Carrot Top Chimichurri* 163
ciabatta: *Pa amb tomàquet* 96
climate change 8, 11–12
coffee grounds 38
community gardens 65, 171
companion planting 37, 144
compost
    homemade 26–7
    ready-made 24–5
compost bins 28
containers 50–1, 73
    attracting pollinators 42
    compost/soil 25
    indoors 70
    making 48–51
    for seeds 48–50
    weight of 72
cooking 54
cordons 94
coriander 37
courgettes 124–7
    Courgette Frittata 127
cream: *Cheesy Leeks with Breadcrumb Topping* 150
crops: deciding what to grow 19–21
cucumber 119–23
    Pickled Cucumber 123
cucumber mosaic virus 122
cuttings: herbs 88

design 76
digging

no-dig gardening 30–1
    tools 22
dips: *Green Pea Dip* 118

egg boxes 48
eggs
    Courgette Frittata 127
    Spanish Tortilla 168–9
eggshells 38
environment 8, 11–12
equipment 22–3
    indoor gardening 69–70

fertiliser 25, 29
flowers 40–3
food waste 25, 26, 54, 60
forks 22
foxes 40
freecycling 171
French beans 111–14
    Lemon and Garlic French Beans 114
frittata: *Courgette Frittata* 127
furniture 47

gardens
    allotments 43, 64, 171
    benefits of 6–8, 11–17
    community gardens 65, 171
    deciding what to grow 19–21
    design 76
    guerrilla gardening 65
    indoor gardening 66–70
    vertical gardening 74–5
garlic 132–6
    Beetroot Hummus 158
    Garlic and Ginger Pak Choi 107
    Lemon and Garlic French Beans 114
    Roasted Garlic Oil 136
    Roasted Radishes with

ABOUT THE AUTHOR

Grace Paul is an editor and writer. She works with some of the world's top publishers as well as leading figures from the food world including chefs, food stylists and photographers.

Teaching herself how to grow vegetables while living in various house shares in London, Grace is proof that you don't need a lot of space or money to grow your own produce. When she's not editing, she can be found cycling around Victoria Park, waging war against slugs in the garden and cooking up her homegrown vegetables.

You can follow Grace on Twitter @gracepaul, Instagram @_grace_paul or see her website www.gracepaul.co.uk.

ACKNOWLEDGEMENTS

It takes a team to create a book and I'd like to thank everyone at Hardie Grant who has played a part in this one. My unreserved thanks and gratitude to Kajal Mistry, for giving me this opportunity and being an absolute dream to work with. Thanks also to Eila Purvis for calmly guiding this book from seed to plant as it were as well as her love of proofreading marks. The beauty of this book is down to two incredibly talented women: Nikki Ellis on design and Rachel Victoria Hillis on the illustrations. Together they've made my words more alive than I could have ever imagined and I'm truly grateful. And last, but not least, thanks to all of the gardeners I've met over the years who've made me laugh over a cuppa, imparted their wisdom and taught me a thing or two about keeping vegetable plants alive.

Published in 2021 by Hardie Grant Books,
an imprint of Hardie Grant Publishing

Hardie Grant Books (London)
5th & 6th Floors
52–54 Southwark Street
London SE1 1UN

Hardie Grant Books (Melbourne)
Building 1, 658 Church Street
Richmond, Victoria 3121

hardiegrantbooks.com

British Library Cataloguing-in-Publication Data.
A catalogue record for this book is available from
the British Library.

The Urban Vegetable Patch
ISBN: 978-1-78488-427-7

10 9 8 7 6 5 4 3 2 1

Publisher: Kajal Mistry
Editor: Eila Purvis
Editorial Assistant: Alexandra Lidgerwood
Design and Art Direction: Nikki Ellis
Illustrations: Rachel Victoria Hillis
Copy-editor: Nikki Duffy
Proofreader: Pami Hoggatt
Indexer: Cathy Heath
Production Controller: Katie Jarvis

Colour reproduction by p2d
Printed and bound in China by Leo Paper Products Ltd.